Ann Sutton

The Crafts Council
in association with Lund Humphries

Ann Sutton

Diane Sheehan
and Susan Tebby

The Crafts Council
44a Pentonville Road
London N1 9BY
www.craftscouncil.org

in association with

Lund Humphries
Gower House
Croft Road
Aldershot
Hampshire GU11 3HR

and

Suite 420
101 Cherry Street
Burlington
VT 05401
USA

www.lundhumphries.com

Lund Humphries is part of Ashgate Publishing

British Library Cataloguing-in-Publication Data
A catalogue record for this book is available from the British Library

ISBN 0 85331 885 9

Library of Congress Control Number: 2003104037

Ann Sutton © The Crafts Council 2003
Text © 2003 the authors

Designed by Chrissie Charlton & Company
Project Management by Rose James
Typeset by Tom Knott
Printed in Singapore under the supervision of MRM Graphics Ltd

frontispiece
1 Ann working on a
miniature textile on a frame
made for her by Jim
Partridge *c.*1981
Photograph: Frank Youngs

Contents

Show5 project initiated by
the Crafts Council

Funded by

Participating galleries

Birmingham Museums
  & Art Gallery
The City Gallery, Leicester
Crafts Council, London
Manchester Art Gallery
The Potteries Museum
  & Art Gallery, Stoke-on-Trent

Foreword

This book is one of a series of five developed as part of the *Show5* partnership initiated by the Crafts Council. *Show5* is the largest collaborative venture between five British museums and galleries, each focusing on the work of one of five leading makers who have helped define the territory of contemporary craft. The aim of this project is to celebrate the impressive achievements of these ground-breaking individuals who have both shaped and influenced the modern craft movement during the past 30 years. Their creative developments and innovative voices are documented and promoted here for an international readership.

The five artists invited to participate work with a wide range of craft media: Carol McNicoll's highly patterned and darkly humorous ceramics; Jim Partridge's pioneering woodwork, which ranges from vessels and furniture to large-scale architectural works; Michael Rowe's complex geometric metalwork; Richard Slee's 'Neo-Pop' ceramics; and Ann Sutton's innovative and experimental woven textiles.

What they do have in common is a desire to expand the boundaries of their craft and take it beyond the conventional and expected. They may, like Slee, McNicoll and Rowe, use traditional techniques to create a style of work that is instantly recognisable. Or, they may employ unusual techniques, like Partridge who uses blowtorches and chainsaws to sculpt his material or Sutton who utilises computer-driven looms.

Show5 is sincerely grateful to the National Touring Programme (Arts Council of England) and Esmée Fairbairn Foundation who have generously supported this creative project. Our thanks also go to Lund Humphries and the writers who had the vision to see the potential for this craft series and with whom we are very pleased to be working. *Show5* would like to thank the five partner galleries, the five artists, the lenders and all those who have contributed their time, ideas and support. A special mention to Kate Brindley and John Williams, without whose energy, commitment and support the project would not have been possible.

Louise Taylor
Director, Crafts Council

Introduction

I work in the technique of weaving, sometimes as an artist, sometimes as a designer, sometimes as a craftsperson. I would starve if I just concentrated on fine art, so I am doing all three, and I find they complement each other. Besides, I don't think you will find anyone else mad enough to tackle them all.

Ann Sutton 1986

This quote from Ann Sutton encapsulates her robust attitude to her work. She has no time for pigeonholing – either of herself or her creations. In an artistic career which spans some fifty years, Ann Sutton's astonishing CV covers product prototyping, working with industry, unique commissions for architects and creating one-off objects – not to mention project management and several international lecture series.

Ann Sutton's practice moves from miniature textiles to large-scale hangings and uses materials as diverse as silk, wool, metal thread, nylon monofilament and perspex. She has invented many innovative techniques for working with textiles and was one of the first practitioners in her field to realise the true potential of computers in creating loom-woven textiles. Her work can be seen worldwide in both public and private collections, most notably the Crafts Council Collection, the Victoria and Albert Museum and the Borås Textilmuseet, Sweden, and she has exhibited in numerous national and international exhibitions.

A distinguishing feature of Sutton's philosophy is her desire to continuously develop and look towards the future. A typical example of this philosophy is her recent initiative, the Ann Sutton Foundation. Launched in 2002, it aims to provide support and resources for three weave fellows while they build their relationships with industry and explore computer-aided weave research. This combination of the practical and innovative exemplifies Ann Sutton's approach to life as well as her work.

The Crafts Council is delighted to be working with Ann Sutton and to have the opportunity to show the diversity and breadth of her career in this, her first full-scale retrospective

2 **Counted Weave** *c.*1969
Perspex sheet and nylon
monofilament.
One of a series of six.
60 x 60 cm; 24 x 24 in
Photograph: Bill Philips

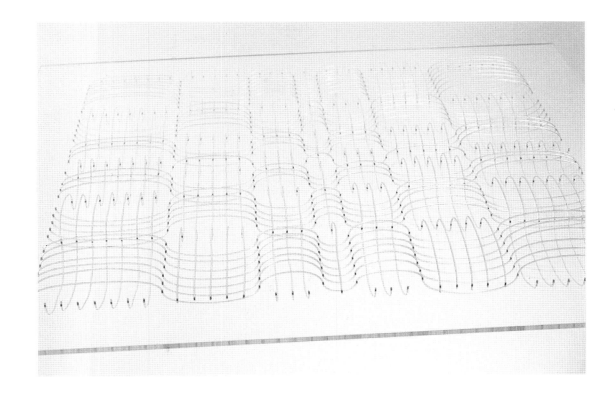

exhibition and its accompanying publication. The exhibition will look closely at the developments Sutton has made in her field: from inventing a macro yarn made on a sock machine, which she used to 'weave' furniture, to her current exploration of high-tech weaving techniques. The variety is hardly surprising given that this is a woman who once said, 'The more hurdles the better – I don't like running on the flat with the wind behind me'.

The Crafts Council would like to express its thanks to Ann Sutton, who has been an inspiration to work with and whose enthusiasm and commitment has contributed so much to the success of this project.

The Crafts Council is grateful to Professor Diane Sheehan and Professor Susan Tebby for their insightful and inspirational contributions to this publication and to David Cripps for his photography. Finally a special mention for Julia Ravenscroft and Angie Hudson whose assistance in organising the exhibition has been invaluable.

We would also like to acknowledge the generosity of all the institutions and private individuals who have loaned work to the exhibition.

Louise Clark
Exhibitions Manager

Ann Sutton
Diane Sheehan

3 **Meadow** 1962
Woven wool warp
with cellophane weft.
Warp-dyed.
210 x 180 cm; 83 x 71 in
Collection: Peter Hauffé
Photograph: Ann Sutton

There is a conceptual core to woven textiles based on the physical structure of weaving that holds the elements of craft, art, design and manufacturing together in a unity: woven structures and woven designs are based on rule-directed processes.

(Peter Dormer (ed.), *The Culture of Craft***, Manchester University Press, Manchester and New York, 1977, p.171)**

Clarity, boldness, wit and logic are the most apparent and enduring hallmarks of Ann Sutton's work. She uses the particular architecture inherent in woven cloth as a basic vocabulary from which she has built her personal language through the imposition of syntactic rules. It may seem peculiar to say that the mind of a weaver is evident in all of Sutton's work, but it is a fact that not every type of textile expresses the logic of weaving. Embroidery (the discipline within which Sutton began her career) allows thread the freedom to intersect pre-woven cloth in any direction and in a variety of stitch forms to 'draw' virtually any image. Likewise, tapestry (a much abused textile term, which in its true form provided the historical precedent for the field of art textiles) uses a passive and invisible warp as a blank page upon which many wefts of differing colours can be worked back and forth with great freedom to create any image. As if involved with another species of fabric entirely, the 'weave-thinking' so apparent in Sutton's work is bound by rules and numbers. The over/under, positive/negative, 1/0 of woven cloth provide the inevitable rules within which a weaver of a more or less 'balanced' cloth (one in which both warps and wefts are visible on the interlaced surface) must operate.

In contrast to the elemental character of her art work, Ann Sutton's 50-year career has been complex and multifaceted, including roles as artist, designer, educator, author, consultant, curator, promoter and organiser. Her life as an artist traces the trajectory of 'craft' from the 1950s, when an occupation in the crafts involved the production of interesting and unique work that relied heavily on history and function for its justification, to the amorphous and effusive entity 'the crafts' have become in the twenty-first century. Today art, craft, design,

4 Grandma Fox (left) and
  daughter Margaret (right)
  in Paris 1908

5 Aunt Margaret Fox of
  Longton, Staffs on
  Mont Blanc, Switzerland
  September 1909

material culture and visual culture are far more intertwined and politicised than they were in the mid-1950s.

Very early on in her career Ann Sutton challenged orthodox notions, categories and boundaries. A keen wordsmith, Sutton has generally avoided the word 'craft' in reference to her work. She prefers the word 'maker' to 'craftsman/woman/person', not least because 'maker' solves the gender problem, but also because the word is forthright, active and has no association with kitschy objects made in profusion by amateurs. The term 'fibre art' has also been considered problematic for its euphemistic definition by medium, which does not quite work when perspex sheets, monofilament, or paint are included as materials. 'Fibre art' also suffers from an over-insistence on being considered art, an issue that Sutton confronted and conquered in the 1960s when she saw the link between the thinking of constructivist artists and the rules of textile construction. Sutton's life and work keep her outside and above definition. Her multifaceted career and her clear yet fluid thinking about the nature of cloth and cloth construction have challenged many superficial assumptions.

Formative years

Sutton's professional life and personal story are so totally intertwined that anecdotal and biographical information cannot be separated from her artistic development. Born in 1935 in North Staffordshire, England, she was a long-awaited only child. Her maternal grandmother provided a model for a strong, self-sufficient, creative businesswoman. Grandmother Fox was a dress designer and maker who travelled to Paris to keep abreast of the newest designs. Judged to be guilty of 'knocking off' Parisian designs, she was often evicted from pavements by employees of couturier establishments for sketching fashions worn by wealthy customers as they emerged from the shops. Her business thrived owing to her tenacity, good taste, willingness to purchase truly fine fabric and her organisational abilities. Successful enough to have as many as 60 seamstresses employed in her workshop, she was the main support of a family headed by an ineffectual patriarch. Of the three Fox daughters, the youngest child (who was to become Mrs Sutton) was the least interested in the dress trade.

6 Ann Sutton aged
about three
Weston Coyney,
Stoke-on-Trent, Staffs

She left it to her only daughter, Ann, to acquire and practise any necessary sewing skills on her own. The middle sister, Elsie, continued in the dressmaking trade with an exclusive, high-end dressmaking studio, though she proved not to be as competent a businesswoman as her mother had been.

A bright, wilful and intensely engaged child, Sutton's earliest memories are tied to the dressmaking workshops owned and managed by Elsie French (née Fox). Lacking siblings, Sutton's ability to invent her own amusements developed early. Even before she was able to walk, she remembers having been placed on the floor in front of the full-length mirror in the fitting room. As she tired of her own image in the mirror, she was handed the only diversion available – a book of textile samples. The first page held an undistinguished fabric of solid navy blue; the second had the same blue fabric but this time with vertical white pinstripes; the third page displayed a fabric with pinstripes in both directions, forming a window pane check. Intrigued by the progression, Ann went back and forth through these pages absorbing the progressive logic, which obviously made a lasting impression.

Another crystalline memory emerges from the war years when toys were very scarce. In a story reminiscent of the 'gifts' developed by the nineteenth-century kindergarten pioneer Friedrich Froebel, Ann remembers a box of 12 brightly coloured felt squares. Froebel's programme (influential in the developing sensibilities of Frank Lloyd Wright, Joseph Albers, Wassily Kandinsky and Piet Mondrian)[1] involved the manipulation of simple geometric shapes and primary colours, which were to be used in systematic play in order to reveal the unity and interconnectedness of the universe. Though Froebel and his theories were unknown to the Sutton family, the basic underlying principles and key aesthetic philosophies seem to be in harmony with the development of modern art in general, and the art of Ann Sutton in particular. Rather than use the fabrics to make dolls' clothes, as was the donor's intention, Ann spent many hours working on the arrangement and rearrangement of these simple, three-inch squares of colour. Only one unhappy memory remains from this game: one of the squares had been trimmed on one side so that it was not truly square and another was slightly thinner than the rest. Ann was annoyed (as Froebel would have been) by these imperfections.

With no apparent aptitude for mathematics and failing to see the relevance of Latin, school was only interesting so long as Sutton was allowed to substitute art and craft activity for academic studies. She won top prizes for her artwork throughout her school years. Having grown up in North Staffordshire, the pottery district, and with a maternal family connection to Aynsley China, a career as a potter seemed a natural choice for Sutton as she applied to art college at the age of 16. For preceding generations of the Sutton family, the job of 'paintress' in the pottery had been a fine career for any young woman with artistic talent. Enrolling for the pottery course at Cardiff College of Art in 1951 seemed an obvious path to a career for Sutton, but she had little practical knowledge of the physical nature of clay. A brilliant and engaging raconteur, Sutton has often described, with delightful wit, her initial encounter with clay and her subsequent decision to enter the embroidery course as a means of escaping the unpleasant messiness of the pottery studio and the repugnant sensation of clay under her fingernails. During her third year as a student of embroidery she was obliged to take a course in another area in order to fulfil the requirements of her programme of study. The dry, countable craft of weaving seemed the only attractive choice. Reluctantly, under the guidance of Kathleen Tarr, Sutton was exposed to rigorous industrial methods of pattern drafting and weave design. Embroidery began to seem superficially decorative in comparison to weaving where the form emerged in an architectural way from the cloth structure. The basis was laid for many ideas Sutton would later come to rely upon.

Following the award of her diploma in 1956 Sutton entered a world in which professional craftswomen were virtually unknown. Only two career paths seemed viable: taking a job in 'a back street factory in Bolton designing for the textile trade' or applying for a teaching position. At age 21 Sutton started teaching at West Sussex College of Art in Worthing, where she was put in charge of the Weave Department. Sutton, not much older than her students at the time, established a collegial, experimental atmosphere in a weave course

7 Ann Sutton working at her
first loom in Sompting,
West Sussex 1958

8 **Woven–Pre-woven** *c.*1964
Jute and perspex.
Approximately 127 x 36 cm;
50 x 14 in

mainly geared toward the production of functional textiles. Exploration of non-traditional materials for weaving was facilitated by the availability of materials used in other workshops. Sutton's attitudes were in tune with the thrust toward breaking old rules and media restrictions, which fuelled the development of the Art Textile movement.

With the realisation that her paper credentials put her at the bottom of the pay scale, and feeling that she needed more time in her own studio, Sutton left West Sussex College in 1963 to seek a part-time position, which would actually pay more and come without full-time faculty responsibilities. An inquiry about the weave course at Croydon revealed that Enid Marx, RDI (1902–98)[2] – whom Sutton had 'worshipped' since age seven when, with her own money, Sutton had purchased one of Marx's books – had just been hired, at age 64, as head of the Textile and Fashion Department. Sutton was hired to revive a defunct weave studio housed in a run-down annexe in which painting, overseen by Richard Allen and Bridget Riley, and graphic design under Herman Hecht were also taught. With the stimulation of other artists and the encouragement of Enid Marx, Sutton found the freedom to try new ideas. In 1965 Sutton proposed and Marx approved a plan to run a short course for fine art weaving during the Easter holidays. It was possibly the first such course in Britain.

Some of her earliest weavings from the period (1956–64) consist of diaphanous woven surfaces incorporating wefts of perspex or acetate with warps of natural fibres. These pieces have a poetic, physical frailty with allusions to natural forms. They bear a similarity to Sutton's early embroideries in their sense of layering and allusive representation. Not entirely divorced from function, there remains the suggestion of curtain or room divider, because they are best seen suspended in space, rather than hung on the wall.

9 Ann as a student at
Barry Summer School
1962

Theoretical base

During her early teaching career Sutton recognised that she needed to learn more about tapestry (a subject not included in her diploma course) in order to teach the subject effectively. She enrolled in a course taught by Tadek Beutlich[3] at the Glamorgan Summer School, Barry, South Wales. There the art world, as opposed to technical craft training, was revealed to Sutton with huge consequences for her work. This was a potent time and Sutton was ready, referring to her education at Barry as 'really the beginning of my life'.

The Barry Summer School, based roughly on the precepts of the Bauhaus,[4] had departments of crafts, painting, music and language, and encouraged interaction, introspection and the examination of post-war art movements. Having been exposed to the excitement generated in other courses offered at Barry while studying tapestry with Beutlich, Sutton enrolled during the subsequent summer in the Basic Design Course under the inspired teaching of Harry Thubron[5] and his team, including Eric Atkinson[6] and Terry Frost.[7] Now recognising how much had been left out of her art school training, she went on to devour theories of colour and space, all the while searching for a method by which she could apply these principles to woven form.

When Beutlich decided to give up teaching at Barry, Sutton was offered the opportunity to teach loom weaving. Finding the looms to be totally inadequate but wanting desperately to teach at Barry, Sutton devised a course based on pure structure, which could be accomplished without the burden of the broken-down looms. Essential textile processes, such as knitting, netting, knotting and darning were used as the bases for constructions executed in a variety of highly experimental materials. The results attracted the attention and admiration of the fine arts tutors who recognised the sculptural and intellectual veracity of Sutton's ideas. She would maintain her fascination with very basic textile structures throughout her career. In fact, until the late 1980s these were the processes she came to rely on most.

10 Teaching at Barry Summer
    School *c.*1966
    The artist Polly Binns is the student
    on Ann's right.
    Photograph: George Lewinski

The evening social life and informal discussions at Barry provided as much of a draw for
Sutton as the intellectual stimulation of the courses. She found the constructivist artist
Kenneth Martin, who taught a sculpture class, to be an excellent dance partner. Mary
Martin,[8] known for her relief constructions, approved of this arrangement since she preferred
not to dance. One summer, for lack of other options, Ann enrolled in Kenneth Martin's
sculpture course expecting a convenient pretext for enjoying the social life at Barry. She was
astonished to find how closely Martin's constructivist ideas about sculpture corresponded to
her own understanding of the nature of woven structures. Martin confirmed for Sutton that
woven structures were a viable medium through which to explore the act of construction for
its own inherent aesthetic.

Kenneth Martin (1905–84) began working on kinetic constructions in 1951.[9] The Martins
are associated with Constructivism, originally a Russian utopian movement, which promoted
mass production through machines as a means of redistributing societal wealth.
Constructivist sculpture was engineered or built mechanically, rather than carved
subtractively. Constructivists were dedicated to the use of the most modern materials –
plastics, glass, metals – which in the past had been considered unaesthetic and therefore
inappropriate art media. Abstract, elemental shapes (spheres, cubes and rectangles), which
are easily made by machine, provided a means to explore the relationship between solids
and voids. Related to Minimalist and Conceptual Art in the United States, the Constructivist

11 **Green Shoots** (detail) 1960
Rep weave, wool and cotton.
179 x 49 cm; 68.5 x 19 in
Collection: Ann Sutton
Photograph: Ann Sutton

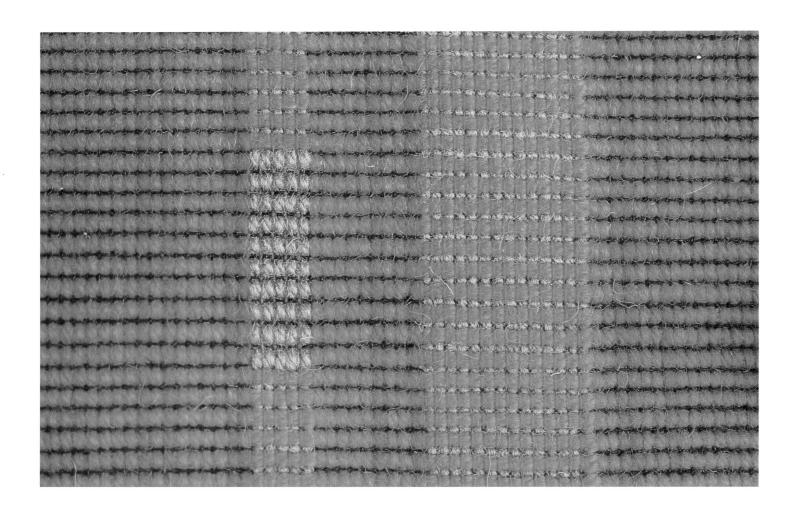

movement had, in contrast, a strong emphasis on social concerns. It was only later that the movement became a political one.

With her natural aversion to the romantic, emotive and messy, the clarity and immediacy of the concepts espoused by Martin, so intrinsically linked to the act of producing cloth on the loom, appealed to Sutton immensely. The establishment of rules and restrictions, often initially dictated by the equipment, and further attenuated by constrictions imposed by each successive decision made by the weaver, became an exhilarating challenge for Sutton. Now, with the conceptual link between sculpture and textile firmly established, she could easily straddle the divide that still existed between fine art and craft in the 1960s. Sutton continued to either attend or teach the summer sessions at Barry throughout the decade, strengthening her resolve and her artistic philosophy.

In the United States during the 1960s a sense of excitement and limitless potential for creative expression energised artists. Art schools and university art departments were booming, filled to capacity, first by GIs who took advantage of post-war educational opportunities afforded to veterans and then, beginning in the 1960s, by their children, the baby boomers. New media such as print-making and the crafts came into the art curriculum. Influential European émigrés, most notably Bauhaus artists Joseph and Anni Albers, brought a modernist, abstract aesthetic and fresh appreciation for the 'designer-craftsman' ideal to North America. Abstract Expressionism's formal freedom and a concurrent movement towards technical experimentation infused American textile art. By Sutton's account, her first awareness of American textile art came in 1963, when, having established herself as writer and contributor to the quarterly *Journal for Weavers, Spinners and Dyers* (she was a also a member of the Editorial Committee), Sutton was asked to review the *Modern American Wall Hangings* exhibition presented at the Victoria and Albert Museum.

A very different art textile aesthetic was emerging from eastern Europe at the time. Led by the Polish Ministry of Arts and Culture, which lent support to the revival of the traditional rug-weaving centre in the north of Poland and the important centre for tapestry weaving in Cracow, eastern Europe developed a stunning new form of textile art. Bold in scale, devoid of representational images, aggressively textured and natural in colour, east European textiles were largely based on the explosion of textile structure to a macrocosmic scale. They were both modernist in the way they allowed form to grow from structure and expressionist in their overwhelming texture and organic form.[10]

The only apparent influence of the new textiles on Ann Sutton's work was eventually manifested in issues of scale and structure. By 1964 the soft colours and poetic transparency of her early weavings began to fall away. Her lack of interest in the emotional appeal of highly textured surfaces inoculated her against overwrought, organic surfaces favoured by east Europeans. The relative isolation of British artists in the post-war years (American craft and design magazines were unavailable in Britain) allowed the two most prominent and quintessentially British textile artists, Ann Sutton and Peter Collingwood, to develop strong, individual artistic voices without much interference from abroad. Working in tandem, with great originality and respect for each other, both Collingwood and Sutton reflect two basic characteristics of British artists: 'moderation on the one hand, wildness on the other'.[11]

Sutton's particular conceptual and formal philosophy, which grew out of her knowledge of Constructivism combined with her interest in structure and scale, set her apart from all other artists of her time. Sutton is opposed to aesthetic choices in art-making. Compositional decisions based on the rules of design, she reasons, are the route to creating palatable objects rather than art. Number systems and decisions based on rules are the only methods by which art can emerge. In her insistence on this dogma, it would seem that Sutton has completely internalised and synthesised both constructivist theory and weave technology: 'I wanted to be controlled by the system. I could then sit back to see what happened. I didn't want to judge. And sometimes I found the results to be visually unpleasant; but that was my problem, not the fault of the art work.'[12]

12 Woven Pendants *c.*1964

Double cloth constructions woven in mercerised cotton with geometric blocks of wood. Ann intended the selvedge of the cloth to be the main feature, so they were displayed with the edge facing the viewer.
Various sizes.
Photograph: Maureen McLeod

In this sense, even when she constructed pieces by hand, she would operate as if she were a loom or, perhaps more accurately, a computer program. The American conceptual artist Sol Lewitt[13] (whom Ann discovered much later and pitied for the fact that he had not taken up weaving) was also working in the same systematic way to produce wall paintings, sculptures and drawings. Like Lewitt, Sutton's working process, begun in the early 1960s, seems to have predicted the computer-dominated world of the twenty-first century. Also like Lewitt, Sutton used this rule-driven way of working to disengage herself from the actual process of making. In a nod to the utopian goals of the Russian constructivists (and perhaps with the business sense of Grandmother Fox tucked in her genes), Ann's working process, governed by rules rather than the sensitive judgements of the artist, meant that the actual construction of the work could easily be left to others.

Professional stance

For the 1965 exhibition of British textiles, *Weaving for Walls* at the Victoria and Albert Museum, Sutton exhibited two works. The more significant of the two, *Woven Pendants* (1964) (12), is possibly the earliest indication of Sutton's wild side. As a challenge to the penchant of British weavers to be overly concerned with technical matters, Sutton decided to make a piece that had the selvedge (the integrity of which was always of utmost concern to hand weavers and the subject of much discussion) as its main feature. She wove a three-inch wide strip of weaving, which alternated between single and double-woven areas, with cleanly geometric blocks of wood inserted in the spaces between the separate planes created by the double structure. The piece was hung perpendicular to the wall (in a challenge to the exhibition's title?) with the edge of the weaving towards the viewer. This is a signature example of Sutton's brand of weave polemics. It may also be the earliest example of her elemental method of handling the woven interaction of primary colours. The warp, made up of one layer of yellow and one layer of red, blended to orange where the two layers came together to make one. *Pendant* is also an important marker of the initial professional collaboration between Ann Sutton and the furniture designer John Makepeace.[14] The original red and yellow Pendant was purchased by the Victoria and Albert Museum.

above left

13 Ann crocheting one of a
    series of three chandeliers
    *c.*1969
    Photograph: Sam Sawdon

above right

14 **Chandelier** *c.*1969
    Knitted polypropylene.
    100 x diam. 45 cm; 39 x 16 in
    Photograph: Sam Sawdon

right

15 **Hanging Lights** 1969
    Knitted linen and nylon
    monofilament with glass inserts.
    Photograph: Sam Sawdon

16 **Knit Structure** 1969
Graded cotton twine on board.
49 x 52 cm; 19 x 20.5 in
Collection: Ann Sutton
Photograph: Sam Sawdon

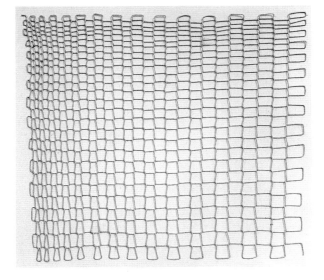

17 **Four Fields Rotating** 1969
Perspex and nylon monofilament.
61 x 61 cm; 24 x 24 in
Collection: Ann Sutton
Photograph: Bill Philips

Sutton and Makepeace married in 1964 and settled into a converted home, gallery and workshop complex reconstructed from a group of farm buildings near Banbury, known as Farnborough Barn. Energised by their common belief in innovation and experimentation, Sutton and Makepeace made a number of collaborative pieces in the 1960s with Sutton designing, creating and sometimes applying soft surfaces to Makepeace's designs; but the primary focus for both artists continued to be their individual development. Some of the most revolutionary and inventive work of Sutton's career, and some of the most modern furniture concepts of Makepeace's career[15] were developed at Farnborough Barn.

In an act of rebellion against the predominance of 'tapestry' as the only true textile art form, during the mid-1960s Sutton began to use common and devalued textile structures such as lace knitting, darning and crochet, exploding the scale to emphasise the magnificence and ingeniousness of their structures. Sutton further defied common art and design tastes of the time by executing these basic textile techniques in 'materials with no history'. She sought out and explored new fibres and old industrial materials: extruded florescent filaments, plastic yarns, perspex and anonymous detritus such as blown glass forms discarded by the navy. The latter became the weights and armatures used to transform knitted tubes of polypropylene, linen, cotton and nylon monofilament into chandeliers (14). Others in the United States and Europe were experimenting with macro textile structures at the time, but Sutton, concentrating on her own ideas, was far too busy to put her head up and look around.

So free was Ann's thinking during this period, so varied her ideas and so prolific her output, she managed to confound (as she still does today) some in her textile art-consuming audience, who are more accustomed to artists who follow a more straight and narrow range of production. Exhibitions in 1969 (*Ann Sutton: Textile Constructions*, British Crafts Centre) and 1970 (*Design 70*, Oxford Gallery) contained works ranging from knitted chandeliers to photo etchings of black nylon stockings, to perspex panels 'stitched' in monofilament. Meanwhile, the singularity of her approach was attracting interest in fine art circles. In a

18 **Slung Sofa** 1966

Wool and wood.
Slung rug seats were a rare combination of Ann Sutton and John Makepeace's work. Wool rug woven by Sutton in Collingwood's double corduroy technique in pink, orange and olive. The frame by Makepeace was made in yew. It had a removable rail for adjustment of the rug if it stretched.
84 x 180 x 75 cm; 33 x 71 x 29.5 in
Collection: Mr and Mrs D Poole
Photograph: Sam Sawdon

19 Solo exhibition at the British Crafts Centre in Covent Garden, London 1969

With perspex maquette for the Welsh Arts Council award-winning sculpture *Bristle Box*.
Photograph: Sam Sawdon

right
20 Interior of Farnborough Barn
*c.*1970

below
21 The Gallery at
Farnborough Barn
Converted from a cart shed by the
architect Graham Anthony.
Photograph: Sam Sawdon

28

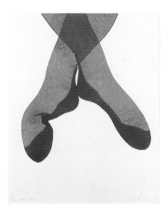

perceptive review of her Oxford Gallery exhibition, Ann's work is described by Marina Vaizey as 'complicated in conception resolved in appearance, totally absorbing to contemplate: austere, fascinating, strikingly individual'.[16] In 1969, a perspex cube pierced through with rods travelling in system-proscribed paths won Sutton the joint first prize in the Welsh Arts Council's *Towards Sculpture* competition and a place in the *National Eisteddfod* exhibition. Once again she used an elemental textile concept (stitching) and her fascination with filaments (line) to produce a work that defied definition.

A sock-knitting machine, well over 100 years old and discovered in a Banbury antique shop in 1967, became the basis for Sutton's most spectacularly innovative work. With this tool, endless tubes of knit material could be produced by anyone who could turn a crank-handle. Sutton saw these tubes as the equivalent of macrofilaments and set out to design her new yarn, which was stuffed with Dacron to keep its dimensions. A loom consisting of stakes driven into the ground in the middle of a field could be made to produce a simple, yet rare textile: a cloth with four selvedges. The darned, plain weave surface was in keeping with Sutton's interest in the most simple textile structures. The resultant *Floor Pad* (1972) (25) was exhibited in the 1973 V&A exhibition, *The Craftsman's Art*. A second experiment involved working the weave around a form to create a square cushion with the beginning and the end of the tubular yarn invisibly grafted to produce an endless structure. The most ambitious of these pieces was *Love Seat* (30), which was commissioned by Liberty's and later bought by the Crown Prince of Qatar. Though its core of foam proved a feat to engineer properly, and the weave required a graft in each warp and weft to eliminate all beginnings and ends, this piece emitted the sense that it had made itself by magic. A perfect synthesis of art, craft and design, it seemed to express a certain British character in its intelligent restraint and witty, wild colour. The enormous tube-knit yarn was to be exploited by Sutton over the next two decades in various sizes, colours and permutations to produce dozens of functional and fine art pieces.

23 **Bristle Box** 1970

Perspex.

Winner of a Welsh Arts Council Sculpture Award.

It was shown at the *Towards Sculpture* exhibition.

274 x 274 x 274cm;

108 x 108 x 108 in excluding plinth

Photograph: Arthur Williamson Studios

24 Sock Machine

The possibilities of the sock machine were introduced into Ann's work in 1967. She would stuff the long tubes of wool 10 cm (4 in) in diameter which it produced, interweave them and then graft the two ends together. This technique was her own invention and she used it to produce cushions, floor mats, pads and chairs. This photograph was taken in 1978.
Photograph: Frank Youngs

25 Floor Pad 1972

Own technique: wool tubing knitted with a sock machine, filled with Dacron and then woven to form a floor pad. It was designed so that the end and beginning of the tubes ended up at the same point and could thus be grafted together invisibly. Unusually it has selvedges on all four sides. Exhibited at *Woven Structures*, Camden Arts Centre (1973) and at *The Maker's Hand* (modified), Victoria and Albert Museum (1975).
430 x 430 x 10 cm; 168 x 168 x 4 in
Photograph: Sam Sawdon

26 Floor Pad (work in progress) 1972

Wool and Dacron.
Stakes in a field were used to lay the warp of the pad. The difficulty of weaving the weft (that is, pulling wool through wool) was overcome by inserting a plastic drainpipe first and then pulling the weft through the pipe.
430 x 430 x 10 cm; 168 x 168 x 4 in
Photograph: Ann Sutton

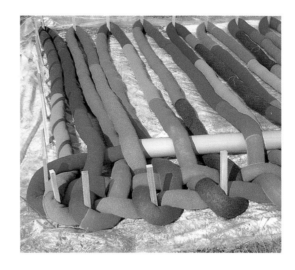

opposite

27 Stand at the *Arkitectur und Wohnen* exhibition, Düsseldorf, Germany *c.*1971

The Ann Sutton and John Makepeace stand at the *Arkitectur und Wohnen (Architecture and Living)* exhibition, Düsseldorf, Germany. The metal tube chair (front left) was designed by John Makepeace and upholstered by Ann Sutton. The cushion/footstool is a chain of spectrum coloured links by Ann Sutton.
Collection (chair): Roy and Rita Harris, Oxford
Photograph: Claus Wolde

28 **Knitweave Armchair** *c.*1976

Wool and Dacron on foam plastic base. Own technique: knitted wool tube, filled with Dacron and then interwoven with the ends grafted together. Similar to the technique used for the *Floor Pad* (25).
73 x 200 x 75 cm; 29 x 39 x 30 in
Collection: Mr and Mrs Malcolm Knapp, New York
Photograph: Sam Sawdon

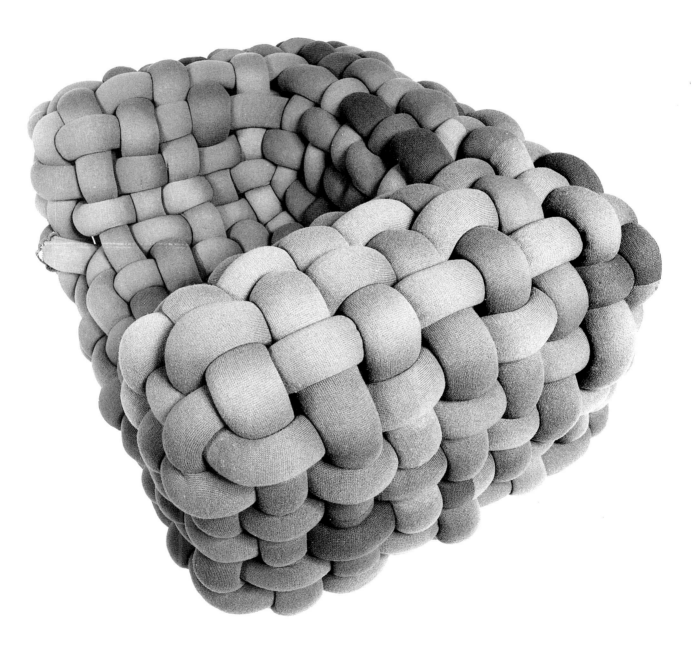

29 Schema for **Loveseat** 1975
Photograph: David Cripps

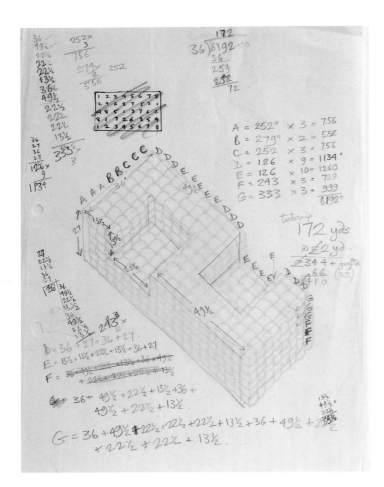

opposite

30 **Loveseat** 1975

Wool, Dacron and plastic foam.
Made using Ann Sutton's own technique:
knitted wool tube filled with Dacron
mounted on a base structure of foams of
varying weight. The interwoven tubes
were grafted together as the ends met the
beginning (36 grafts in total).
Commissioned by Liberty & Co. for their
centenary, *Loveseat* was sold to Cecil Gee
Ltd in Shaftesbury Avenue, where it was
seen by the Crown Prince of Qatar who
bought the shop in order to obtain it.
73 x 170 x 75 cm; 29 x 67 x 30 in
Photograph: Ann Sutton

31 **Ring Chain Spectrum** *c.*1974
Wool and Dacron.
Own technique: knitted wool tubes filled
with Dacron, interwoven and linked with
the ends grafted together.
38 x 86 x 60 cm; 15 x 34 x 24 in
Photograph: Sam Sawdon

opposite
32 **Linked Square Spectrum** 1974
Knitted interwoven wool miniature exhibited
at the *First International Exhibition of
Miniature Textiles*, British Crafts Centre,
London and world tour.
18.5 x 18.5 cm; 7 x 7 in
Photograph: David Cripps

33 Unit Textiles *c.*1974

Drawings of invented semi-skilled techniques
for production in the studio at Mollington.
Photograph: David Cripps

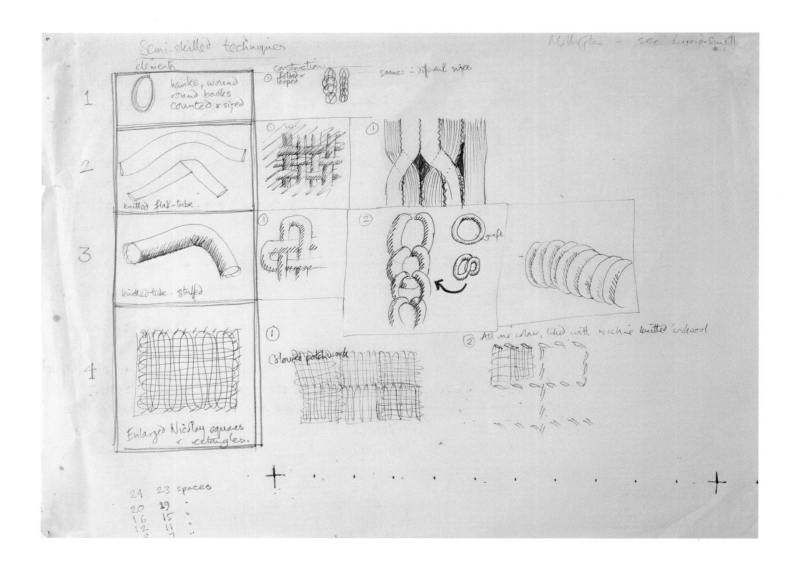

34 Interior of Mollington
Workshop, The Old Chapel
October 1974
Work in progress, from front: small
Floor Pad, padded mohair bed
cover and knitted hanging
(first row in progress).
Photograph: Ann Sutton

In order to increase her production, Sutton organised an independent workshop in which she could employ workers without textile skills who could execute her many ideas. A chapel in Mollington, north of Banbury, was converted for this purpose and between 1974 and 1976 Sutton conceived pieces that could be carried out by local, unskilled labour. During this period Sutton specifically designed work based on unitised construction and systematic rules. Cushions, constructed of knitted tubes, woven with the smallest number of warp and weft elements possible, were a major production item. Sutton takes pleasure in the belief that the Mollington enterprise was as much a social benefit as an artistic endeavour. Isolated local housewives found employment, companionship and purpose and Sutton was able to realise many ideas quickly.

Works produced at Mollington include *5 x 5 = 25*, made for the Queen's Silver Jubilee (50), which was woven with only the simplest of pin and board looms, producing darned squares of cloth with four selvedges. In each square the blend of colour is determined by a strict system, eliminating the need for the worker to make decisions. The coloured squares were then linked with almost invisible monofilament squares so that they seem to hover, mysteriously suspended in space. The appeal of this piece lies in the tension put into play by the juxtaposition of dissimilar formal values: the strict geometry of the grid, the elemental simplicity of the plain woven lurex and rayon squares, and the intimate complexity of the blended woven colour. The technique and format appealed to Sutton (she was to create three variants on this theme), not least because the reliance on darned units allowed for pieces to be farmed to outworkers.

35 **Spectrum Link** 1974–5
One of a set of 14 hangings of
linked wool loops, sold separately.
Exhibited at *Ann Sutton – Textiles,*
British Crafts Centre.
182 x 54 x 4 cm; 72 x 22 x 2 in
Collection: Ann Sutton
Photograph: David Cripps

36 Interior of the Mollington
   studio *c.*1974

37 **Spectrum Link Hangings,**
   with **Knot Cushions** in
   foreground 1974–5
   Set of 14 hangings of linked wool
   loops, sold separately.
   Exhibited at *Ann Sutton – Textiles*,
   British Crafts Centre.
   Approximately 182 x 54 x 4 cm;
   72 x 22 x 2 in
   Collections: Crafts Council,
   Professor and Mrs R Harris,
   Ann Sutton
   Photograph: Sam Sawdon

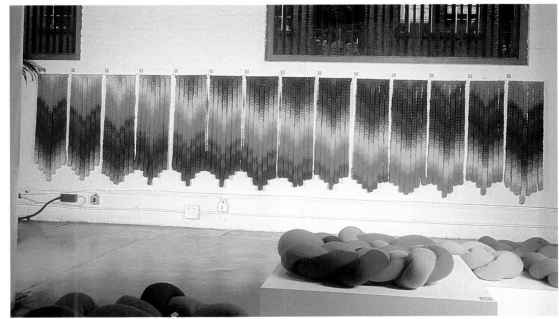

38 Linked Spectrum Rings
1974–5
Jute wrapped with wool.
Diam. 8–13 cm; 3–5 in
Photograph: David Cripps

39 Logical Weave Footstool
1970s

Wool and Dacron.
Own technique: knitted wool tubes in primary and secondary colours, filled with Dacron and interwoven with the ends grafted together.
Diam. 40 cm; 16 in

40 Knot Cushions 1975

Wool and Dacron.
Own technique: knitted wool tubes filled with Dacron and interwoven with the ends grafted together.
All made at the Mollington studio, the lower cushion was produced in quantities, always in two high-saturation colours; the other two were one-off designs.
14 x 48 x 37 cm; 5.5 x 19 x 15 in
Photograph: Sam Sawdon

left

41 **Diamond 1–11** *c.*1974

Wool and Dacron.
Own technique: knitted wool tubes filled with Dacron and interwoven with the ends grafted together. Colours dictated by permutation. Exhibited by the British Crafts Centre in *Contemporary British Tapestry*.
220 x 220 cm; 78 x 86 in
Photograph: David Cripps

right

42 Parnham

The historic house purchased by Ann Sutton and John Makepeace in 1976. It was converted into furniture-making studios and a school for craftspeople in wood.

far right

43 Fig Tree Cottage, Worthing, West Sussex

The workshop (eight-foot square) was to the left of the front door and could only accommodate a 12 inch wide loom.

The move to Parnham, an historic house in Dorset dating from 1190 and purchased by Sutton and Makepeace in 1976, brought a crushing halt to Sutton's workshop and her working rhythm. Renovations to carve out studio, furniture, school and living space, the need to open the house to the public and provide tea and scones in large quantities, and the organisational skills she applied to this huge enterprise consumed her time. Ever the businesswoman at heart, as director of John Makepeace Ltd she found satisfaction in helping to shape the large and multifaceted Makepeace–Sutton interior design, furniture and textile design firm. However, the 15-year partnership ended in 1978 and the marriage was dissolved in 1979. Initially settling into a very small temporary studio ('Fig Tree') where Sutton concentrated on producing cushions of all sorts, she later purchased a handsome but run down Georgian building on Tarrant Street in Arundel, which houses her flat and studio today.

From 1980 onward Sutton's career accelerated as she accepted more diverse opportunities, travelled and taught widely, and solidified her artistic reputation with major museum exhibitions in Sweden, Wales and England (Winchester). The first opportunity presented itself just as Sutton was moving from Fig Tree to Arundel in 1980. The BBC began planning a television series on weaving, called *The Craft of the Weaver*. The shy Peter Collingwood had declined an invitation to be the presenter, affording Sutton the opportunity to both present the series and to write the accompanying book, *Craft of the Weaver*. The series was a hit, Sutton became a British personality and seven books were to follow, establishing her international reputation as a weave authority. Of her books, *The Structure of Weaving* (1982) was perhaps the most revolutionary for its uncommon clarity, its lack of weave recipes, and the amazing life-like photography, which changed forever the look of craft publishing.

44 Pattern design samples
Between 1967 and 1978
Ann Sutton acted as consultant to
various Welsh woollen mills to
modernise their products. These are
samples of her dramatic re-colouring
of traditional designs.
Photograph: David Cripps

45 1–6 Pendulum Permutation
1975
Own technique: unit textile, darned jute
squares hooked with deep wool pile,
assembled by lacing to form a rug.
130 x 130 x 5 cm; 51 x 51 x 2 in
Photograph: Sam Sawdon

46 Number Game – Red, Blue, Yellow
*c.*1975
Cotton threads pierce a perspex sheet,
weave and return to the other side.
Boxed in perspex.
25 x 25 x 7 cm; 10 x 10 x 3 in
Collection: Crafts Council
Photograph: Sam Sawdon

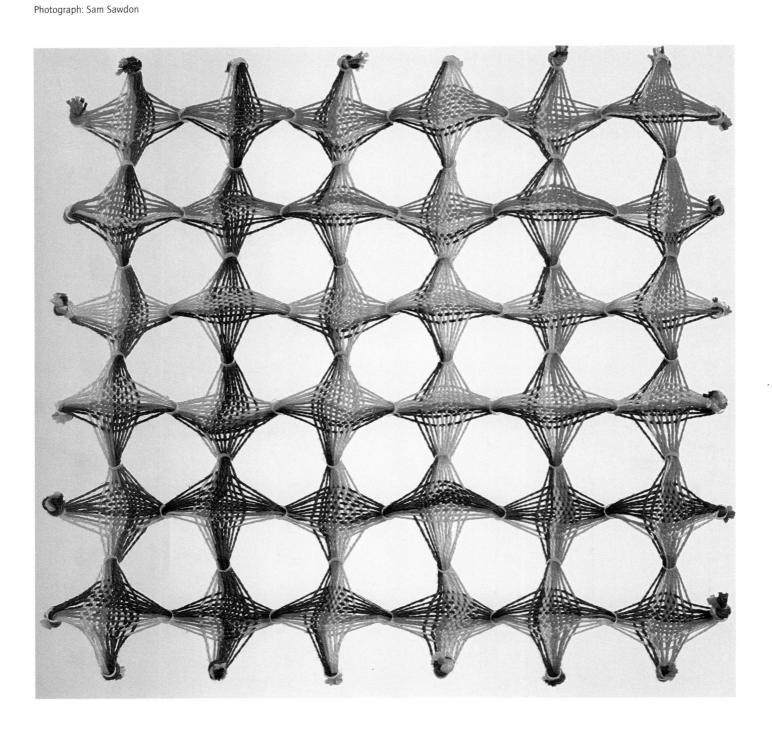

Schema for
47 **Padded Mohair Bed Cover**
1974
Mohair and Dacron.
148 x 148 x 4 cm; 58 x 58 x 2 in
Photograph: David Cripps

48 **Bedcover Mk II** *c.*1976
Mohair and Dacron.
Own technique: darned padded
mohair squares with Dacron
padding, laced together with
space-dyed knitted wool rouleaux.
148 x 148 cm; 58 x 58 in
Photograph: David Cripps

49 **Transition Spectrum Permutation** 1976

Ann Sutton's own technique: darned wool weaves assembled by lacing together with nylon monofilament. The system is a pendulum permutation with cross-pollinated spectrum colouring.
167 x 216 cm; 66 x 85 in
Collection: Lotherton Hall, Leeds
Photograph: Courtesy of Leeds Museums and Galleries

50 **5 x 5 = 25** (detail) 1977

Rayon, lurex and nylon monofilament. Hanging made using invisible square technique. It was made to commemorate the Queen's Silver Jubilee and exhibited by the British Crafts Council.
216 x 167 cm; 85 x 66 in
Collection: Ann Sutton
Photograph: David Cripps

51 **Related pair of cushions**
1979

Machine knitted wool.
Round cushion folds alternating
left/right, left/right. Square cushion
folds spirally on machine during
construction. Both cushions were
sold to Coexistence.
Top: diam. 42 x 16 cm; 17 x 6 in
Bottom: 48 x 48 x 16 cm;
19 x 19 x 6 in

52

below right

52 **Corset Cushion** 1978

A one-off design of knitted and
grafted wool tubes, stuffed with
Dacron and fastened together with
woven woollen squares.
50 x 50 x 10 cm; 20 x 20 x 4 in
Collection: Crafts Council
Photograph: Ann Sutton

53 **1–6 Pendulum
Permutation Cushion** _c._1980
Mohair.
Darned squares laced togther.
50 x 50 cm; 20 x 20 in
Collection: Crafts Council
Photograph: Sam Sawdon

left

54 Woven Knitted Spectrum
1974
Wool.
Knitted interwoven miniature
structure exhibited at the
*First International Exhibition
of Knitted Textiles.*
18 x 18 cm; 7 x 7 in
Photograph: David Cripps

right

**55 Primary Unit Cube and
Primary Unit Square** 1979
Mercerised cotton.
Loom-woven miniatures, constructed
by knotting the warp ends through
the weft loops. Exhibited at the
*Fourth Exhibition of Miniature
Textiles* at the British Crafts Centre.
Both approximately
7.5 x 7.5 x 7.5 cm; 3 x 3 x 3 in
Photograph: David Cripps

below

57 Bracelet 1980

Ann Sutton's own technique:
overlapping squares are darned in
nylon monofilament. Exhibited at *Soft
Wear* at the Arnolfini Gallery, Bristol.
10 x 15 cm; 4 x 6 in
Photograph: Ann Sutton

left

56 Colour Change Net 1981

Wool.

Cord, made in spectrum range and
order, interlocked into a large grid
mesh. The net is intended to be seen
in a heap showing different colour
juxtapositions each time it is dropped.
Size, when in a heap,
40 x 40 cm; 16 x 16 in
Photograph: David Cripps

left

58 Exterior shot of 40 Tarrant
Street, Arundel 1980
With 'Sold' sign.
Photograph: Frank Youngs

right

59 Ann Sutton's Arundel
studio
In the late 1980s, showing a 24-shaft
Compudobby Loom.

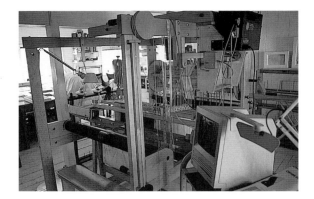

Serial permutations

The intensity of questioning evident in Sutton's work seems to have increased exponentially with each passing decade with the pace of her idea-production. During the 1980s an 'obsession with white' inspired the *Frozen Fabric* series (62–64), works which were constructed of coloured materials and then 'whitewashed' with pigment, stiffening the fabric while nearly obscuring the colour Only hints of the original saturated hues bleed through the painted surface or remain exposed at the edges. Sutton, once again working counter to the commonly accepted nature of cloth, set up allusions to the fine art tradition of painting on canvas. With a quiet defiance against both craft and art, she defaces the cloth she has so painstakingly constructed by hand, and compounds the irony by using paint as a negation of a coloured ground.

Sutton was an early adopter and promoter of computer-aided design/manufacturing (CAD/CAM) weave technology in the 1980s, and took to it as if she had been anticipating its arrival since the 1960s (in fact, she had joined the Computer Art Society in 1964). Now with the ability to weave complex patterns and multiple layers, Sutton has allowed her work to float even more freely between applied design and fine art. She had been weaving small but brilliant studies (more like artists' sketches than industrial samples) on her computer dobby loom for a number of years when she was asked to prepare an exhibition at the Winchester Gallery, Winchester School of Art. Sutton created six series of six pieces, each of which turned the traditional weaving practice of 'sampling' into a treatise on permutation, e.g. *Spectrum Patches* (104). Small squares of cloth were woven to specific computer-guided rules, one after the other in sequence. Some had layers of varying fibres, which were made to take on odd forms after washing. All were presented without editing to make systematic changes in the fabric structure apparent to all. Called *No Cheating*, the 1995 exhibition capitalised on the rule-driven choices imposed by the computer as it controls the loom, and continues the didactic (a quieter form of polemic?) mode Sutton has always favoured in her work.

60 **Three Painted Miniatures: Chenille Diagonal, Linen Diagonal and Wool Diagonal**
1981
Wool, linen and acrylic paint. Experiments in diagonal darning, all painted with white acrylic paint leaving the ends as 'clues' (*Linen Diagonal* is in the collection of Peter Collingwood).
28.5 x 28.5 cm; 11 x 11 in
Photograph: Anders Rydén

61 **Flip Flop Section** (detail)
Woven cotton cloth strip and
acrylic paint.
Loom-woven and embroidered
cotton with acrylic paint.
One of the *Frozen Fabric* series.
181 x 26 cm; 71 x 10 in
Photograph: Ann Sutton

right
62 **Frozen Fabric: Twills**
1983
Woven cotton cloth strip
and acrylic paint.
34 x 24.5 cm; 13 x 10 in
Collection: Ann Sutton
Photograph: David Cripps

63 **Frozen Fabric: Spectrum**
1983
Woven varied fibres and
acrylic paint.
87 x 87 cm; 34 x 34 in
Collection: Ann Sutton
Photograph: Ann Sutton

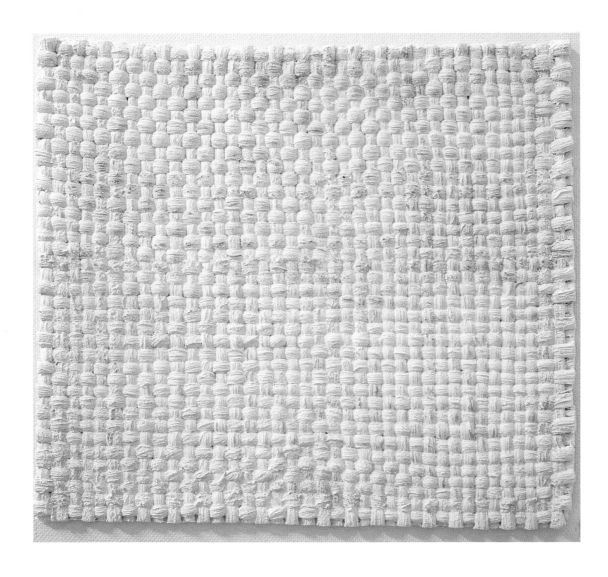

64 **Frozen Fabric: Black & White**
1990s
Cotton cloth strip and acrylic paint.
21 x 21 cm; 8 x 8 in
Collection: Ann Sutton
Photograph: Ann Sutton

65 **Two Landscapes** 1999

Linen and acrylic.
Left: 21 x 9 x 3 cm; 8 x 3.5 x 1 in
Right: 26 x 14 x 3 cm; 10 x 5.5 x 1 in
Collection: Ann Sutton
Photograph: Ann Sutton

66 **Bedcovers** Early 1980s
Powerloom-woven double plain in wool.
Designed for Delaunay (with furniture by
Floris van den Broecke).
240 x 250 cm; 94 x 98 in

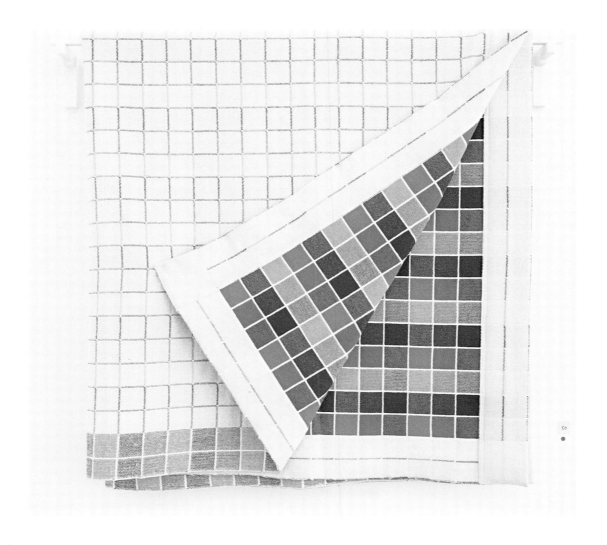

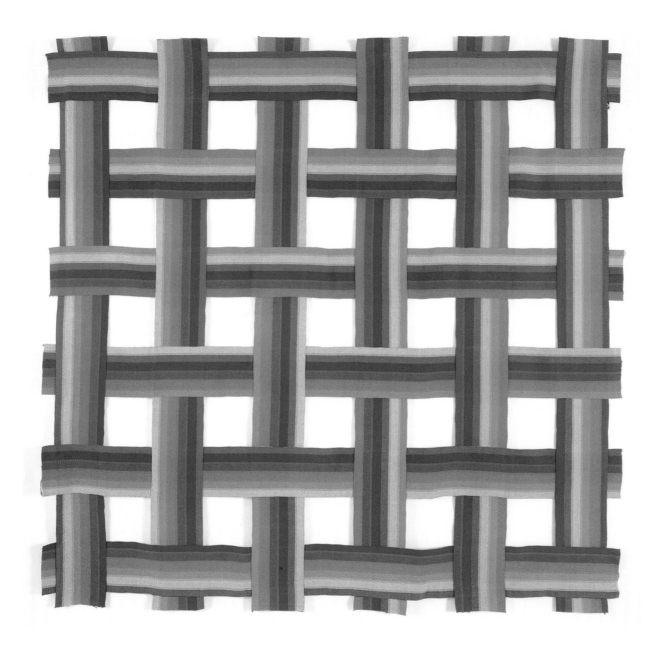

above
67 1-6 Spectrum Bands Rotating 1983
Loom-woven bands of wool in spectrum order, with colours shifting to the left in successive bands.
183 x 183 cm; 72 x 72 in
Photograph: David Cripps

opposite above
68 Bedcovers 1983
Wool.
Powerloom-woven double plain in two colour ways on white ground, the pattern repeat and colour repeat do not coincide for over a metre. The left-hand version has primary colours in the warp and secondary in the weft; the right-hand bedcover used primary colours in both the warp and weft.
267 x 255 cm; 105 x 100 in
Photograph: Frank Youngs

opposite below
69 Powerloom Throw c.1983
Double plain powerloom-woven wool with hand-woven edge.
196 x 124 cm; 77 x 49 in
Photograph: Frank Youngs

70 **Overlaid Meshes** 1983/4
Loom-woven.
Multicoloured wool warp, individual
colours as wefts. Acrylic paint.
44 x 86.5 cm; 17 x 34 in
Photograph: Ann Sutton

71 **Spectrum Interlink Spectrum Bands**
(detail) 1984
Loom-woven bands in wool, linked warp
colouring, folded and stitched.
Hanging exhibited at the Konstmuseum, Norrköpings,
Sweden (solo show) in 1985.
300 x 132 cm; 118 x 52 in
Collection: Konstmuseum, Norrköpings, Sweden
Photograph: Anders Rydén

72 **Cutaway Squares** 1984

Loom-woven wool in spectrum order, with cut holes that
are sealed. This was a set of three weavings exhibited in
Ann's solo show at the Konstmuseum, Norrköpings,
Sweden, in 1985.
96 x 96 cm; 38 x 38 in
Collection: Ann Sutton
Photograph: David Cripps

73 **Cutaway Squares** (detail) 1984

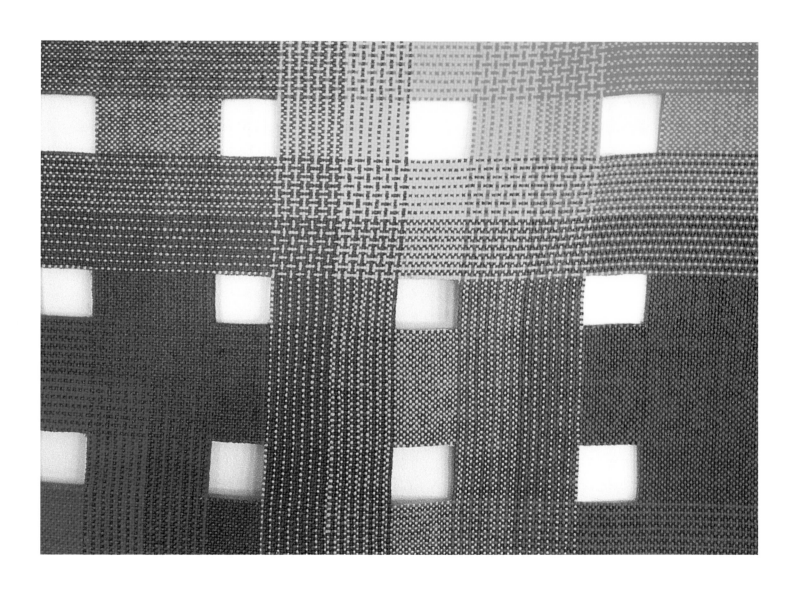

Several other serial themes have emerged during the last decade, most notably an investigation of the satin weave structure. Satin, a weave that is designed according to a particular numerical system, can be made to produce a smooth warp-faced surface or a smooth weft-faced surface (sateen) as in damask. In an interesting allusion to the primeval 'straw into gold' story, Sutton, using a linen warp, a gold weft and a 24-harness computer-driven loom created surfaces that magically transmuted from warp (linen) faced satin to weft (gold) faced sateen. In order to accomplish the illusion of mutation, the weave (a series of satins carefully designed to gradually become sateens) needed to be painstakingly calculated to produce absolutely smooth transitions.

Another ongoing, very low-tech series of 'seismic' drawings (*Movement Meshes*) records the effect of subtle natural forces on a carefully spaced grid of horizontal and vertical lines on paper. Accomplished mainly during ocean voyages (Sutton has travelled to New Zealand by freighter for the past several winters), each line is a record of the roll of the ocean and the vibration of the ship's engines on the artist's hand. Once again Sutton utilises a force beyond the maker to dictate the outcome of the work. Each drawing, subtly distinct in minute detail from the character of all the others, resembles a mesh woven of a highly twisted fibre in which the energy of the yarn generates a lively surface.

Sutton as designer/developer

Throughout her career, Sutton has applied passion, skill and finely honed wit to massive projects of all sorts, which have been accomplished in tandem with her studio art work. Her interest in the magnification of scale and penchant for theatre led her to conceive the 'largest knitted structure in the world', which was to stretch from Oxfordshire to Birmingham (contrived to arrive completed on 1 April 1969). At the request of the BBC for a news item about her current work, Sutton invented a piece that was to be 'knitted' by students, cones on their heads, performing the action of needles on a knitting machine. In October 1984 Sutton was asked to create a work for Quarry Bank Mill, Styal, in Cheshire (a National Trust property). In a bold move, she had the 'largest and fastest (11 minutes 26 seconds) weaving

74 **'The Largest Piece of Knitting in the World'** 1970
A BBC television news feature, conceptually this piece of knitting 'stretched' for 30 miles.

75 **'The Largest, Fastest, Weaving in the World'** 1984
This weaving took 11 minutes and 26 seconds to execute. Each strip was 91 cm wide (i.e. a yard) and each horizontal band was 10.4 metres across and the vertical bands were 29 metres deep. It was part of an installation to celebrate 200 years of Quarry Bank Mill, a National Trust property in Styal, Cheshire.

in the world' constructed from bolts of cloth dyed in her signature primary and secondary colours. On cue, workers stationed at the beautifully spaced windows on the face of the mill dropped warps and interlaced wefts to the cheers of an assembled crowd. Though her maverick stance would prevent her from ascribing to any such movement, these choreographed constructions of exploded textile structure are tongue-in-cheek relatives of the 'performance art' genre.

At the other end of the spectrum, Sutton had instigated the *First International Miniature Textiles Exhibition* in London in 1974. In an act of rebellion against the highly influential Lausanne Biennale exhibition's emphasis on large-scale textiles, Sutton devised an exhibit of works occupying less than 20 cubic centimetres. By legitimising the concept of small-scale textile art (which actually brought the medium back full circle to its 'lap work' tradition) Sutton opened an entirely new avenue of expression for textile artists, making a huge and lasting impact on the field. By 1980, issues of scale seem to have been exorcised from Sutton's own work as she has settled into moderately sized serial investigations of structure.

Consultancies, such as a 1984–5 advisory position to the Welsh woollen industry, were often converted into design projects. Having been asked to assess the state of the Welsh weaving industry, Sutton developed an admiration for the Welsh tradition of substantial double-woven woollen textiles. Along with a range of children's wear, designed by Juliet Mann, Sutton designed a line of furnishing fabrics. Woven bedcovers, bold in scale and colour, combined Sutton's interest in the way primary colours can be weave-blended to produce a myriad of hues with the simple positive/negative block format dictated by the fabric structure. These she had powerloom woven and cut into bed-size coverlets. Later, powerlooms wove throws in red, blue and yellow broadcloth. To add value and distinction, the edges of these were bound with hand-woven bands of the same wool – the only way to achieve a perfect match and proper selvedges.

76 **Primary/Secondary Interweave**

Wool.

The bands, which have warps linked in complementary colours, are loom-woven and then interwoven.

140 x 140 cm; 55 x 55 in

Collection: Borås Textilmuseet, Sweden

Photograph: Ann Sutton

below

77 **Primary/Secondary Interweave** (detail)

Collection: Borås Textilmuseet, Sweden

Photograph: Ann Sutton

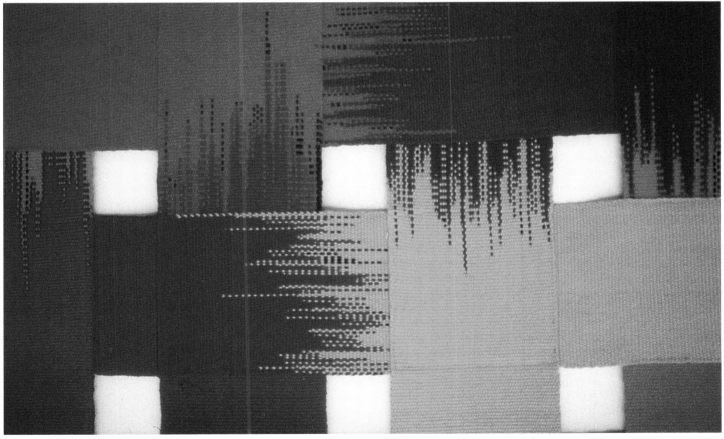

78 Solo exhibition at the
    Konstmuseum,
    Norrköpings, Sweden
    1985
    Showing Ann Sutton's pieced cloth
    banners in spectrum order. Designed
    for the Crafts Council building in
    Waterloo Place, London.
    Photograph: Anders Rydén

79 **Constructivist Clothes**
    1985
    Part of a collection of spectrum-
    coloured silk garments by Ann
    Sutton with Diana Hawkins.
    Exhibited at the Konstmuseum,
    Norrköpings, Sweden (solo show)
    and at the Oxford Gallery with
    Caroline Broadhead in 1985.
    Collection: Ann Sutton
    Photograph: Anders Rydén

Based on Sutton's growing reputation as an artist/organiser, in 1992 the Dean and Chapter of Winchester Cathedral asked her to manage the refurbishing of all ceremonial and decorative textiles throughout the cathedral. Sutton sought proposals from the best artists in Britain, assigning to each a particular chapel or altar. Issey Miyake[17] (b.1938) was brought in to create the vestments. Three chapels have been completed to date, but the necessity to raise funds for other, more pressing, needs of the building has prevented the rest of this visionary project from being realised. Sutton also served as lead organiser for a team of artists and architects working on the award winning conversion of the Eastleigh Town Hall into 'The Point', a dance centre. Sutton's fearless visionary thinking allows her to approach huge projects, which involve a range of interior design, architectural renovation and product design elements, with the eye and mind of an artist.

Sutton has produced freelance CAD/CAM designs for industry during the past 20 years, with US clients such as Polo Ralph Lauren and Fieldcrest Cannon. In collaboration with the Japanese textile designer, Junichi Arai, she produced bridal fabric collections in 1988 and 1989, and also consulted for NUNO textiles of Japan. Her expertise has been sought by the Joseph and Anni Albers Foundation in the United States where she serves as consultant. She has been a judge for both the Swiss Design Prize and the Tokyo Fashion Fabric Design Contest, prestigious international design competitions. For her innovative work in textiles, she was made a Member of the Order of the British Empire (MBE) by HM the Queen in the New Year Honours List of 1991.

As a living synthesis of the various aspects of her multifarious career, Sutton conceived and initiated The Ann Sutton Foundation in 2001 as a research and development laboratory for elevating the quality of woven textiles in industry, art and science. Appointed postgraduate design research fellows work in well-equipped Foundation facilities, where they apply their creative, technical and business skills towards solutions for commissioned projects. Financed by commercial, government and private sources and advised by a board with wide international expertise, the Foundation will take Sutton's concern for talent development and innovative textile solutions into the future.

80 Dancing Figure Permutation 1993

Cotton and wool.
Miniature textile: loom-woven grey and white cotton ground inlaid with wool.
24 x 24 cm; 9 x 9 in
Photograph: David Cripps

81 White, Grey, Red Increasing/Diminishing Bands 1984

Loom-woven cotton in double plain weave: one of an edition of four.
Collection: Ann Sutton
Photograph: David Cripps

78

Though she has continued to teach workshops and short courses throughout her career, the Ann Sutton Foundation provides a formal platform for the dissemination of Sutton's considerable knowledge and experience in textiles. As if consciously applying her design skills to her own life plan, she has managed to bring her career full circle back to her early years as an instructor, now with a more complex and ambitious purpose. (Interestingly, in another nod to the past, one of her very recent series of weavings, reminiscent of landscape and natural form, indicate a certain mellowed return to some of her early woven themes.) As she has throughout her career, Sutton continues to investigate the familiar and humble nature of cloth, and by applying her singular brand of rigour and discipline, manages to turn it into a metaphor for universal order and transformation.

Notes

1 Norman Brosterman, *Inventing Kindergarten,* Harry N. Abrams, New York, 1997, p.13.

2 Enid Marx trained at the Central School for Arts and Crafts and the Royal College of Art. During the 1930s she designed and hand-printed home furnishing fabrics. After the war she concentrated on woven textile designs for industry as well as book jackets, book illustrations and stamps. Along with historian Margaret Lambert, she wrote three books on English popular arts.

3 Tadek Beutlich (b.1922), a Polish-born tapestry weaver whose work was prominent in the 1950s to the 1970s.

4 The Bauhaus, a German art and design academy established in 1919 in Weimar, which honoured craftsmanship, taught design principles common to all art forms, and rejected the notion of art and architecture as ornament.

5 Harry Thubron, 1915–86, was arguably the finest art teacher in the United Kingdom in the twentieth century. With Victor Pasmore, he founded the Basic Design Course at Leeds College of Art, and taught it on short courses (including Barry) throughout the country.

6 Eric Atkinson (b.1928) taught at Leeds as Harry Thubron's right-hand man, then moved to Canada (London, Ontario).

7 Sir Terry Frost RA (b.1915), a British painter, knighted in 1998 and elected to the Royal Academy in 1992. Professor Emeritus, University of Reading.

8 Mary Martin, 1907–69, produced relief sculptures in which geometric elements and their shadows produced monochromatic compositions.

9 Stephen Bann (ed.), *The Documents of 20th Century Art: The Traditions of Constructivism*, Thames and Hudson Ltd, London, 1974, pp 267–8.

10 Mildred Constantine and Jack Lenor Larsen, *Beyond Craft: The Art Fabric*, Van Nostrand Reinhold Company, New York, 1972, p.37.

11 Willy Rotzler, *Constructive Concepts*, Rizzoli International Publications, Inc, New York, 1989, p.187.

12 Taped interview with Dr Mirjana Teofanović, 1997.

13 Sol Lewitt, b.1928. An important American artist associated with the Conceptual and Minimal art movements, noted for sculptures and wall paintings that explore the potential of ideas, chance and intuition to generate visual form.

14 John Makepeace, b.1939. One of Britain's best-known furniture makers. Organised the *Designer Craftsman* 1963 exhibition at the Herbert Art Gallery during which he met Ann Sutton.

15 Tanya Harrod, *The Crafts in Britain in the 20th Century*, Yale University Press, New Haven, 1999, p.405.

16 Marina Vaizey, '*Design 70*, Oxford Gallery' (review), *Arts Review*, 28 February 1970.

17 Issey Miyake attended Tama Art University in Tokyo in the early 1960s and graduated with a degree in Graphic Design. An ambition to become a fashion designer led him to an apprenticeship in Paris. Relying on his Japanese heritage rather than on knowledge of Western fashion, he presented his first collection in Paris in 1973. His revolutionary clothing – more sculpture in cloth than fashion – has been exhibited at museums throughout the world including the Victoria and Albert Museum, London; the Centre Georges Pompidou, Paris; and the Seibu Museum of Art, Tokyo.

82 **Increasing Spectrum Bands**
1986
Cotton.
Miniature textile woven on an early
powerloom in the Borås
Textilmuseet, Sweden, during a
solo exhibition there.
33.5 x 25 cm; 13 x 10 in
Photograph: Ann Sutton

83 **Untitled experimental work** 1993
Cotton and plastic clay.
Based on the primitive stick and
shell maps of Pacific atolls.
26 x 26 cm; 10 x 10 in
Collection: Rosemary Moon

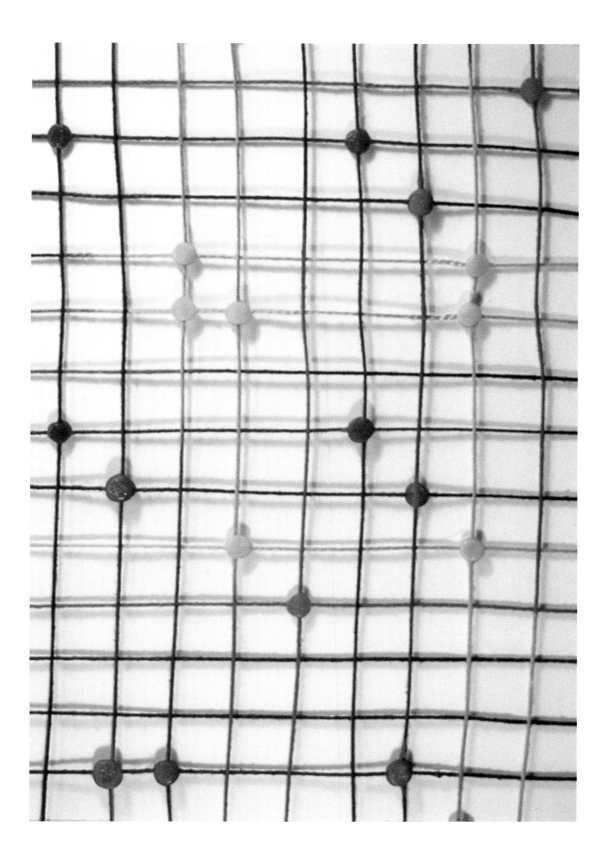

84 **1-6 Pendulum Permutation,
Primary/Secondary Colours
Plus One** 1980s
Linked, darned wool squares.
102 x 102 cm; 40 x 40 in
Collection: Ann Sutton
Photograph: Ann Sutton

85 **Pale Spectrum**
Permutation (detail)
Darned cotton cloth strip with single
coloured thread.
184 x 184 cm; 6 x 6 ft
Collection: Peter and Ursula
Sturzinger, Switzerland
Photograph: Frank Youngs

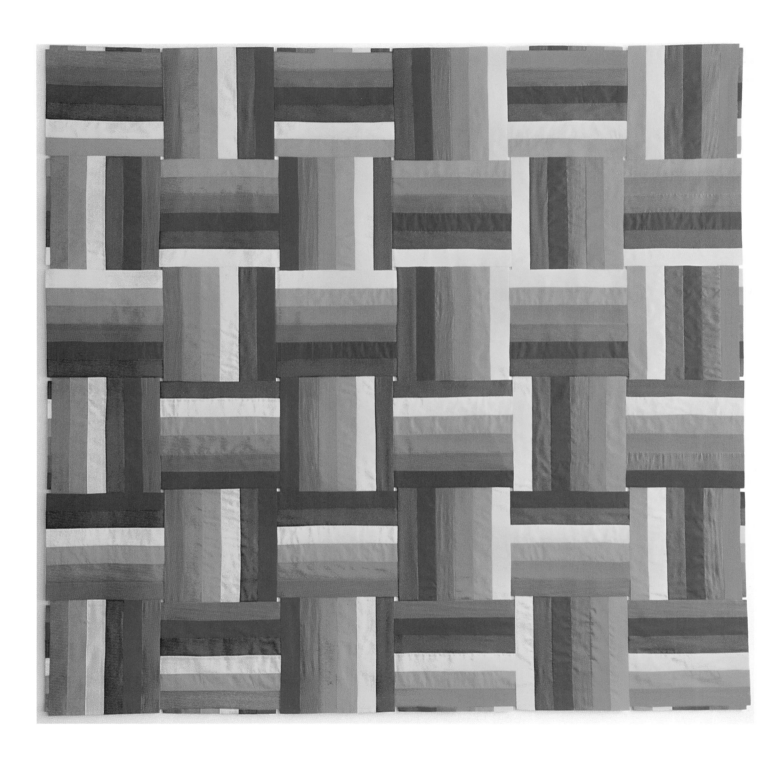

opposite

86 **Rotating Spectrum Bands**
1986
Hanging made of pieced and stitched
interwoven silk fabric bands.
200 x 200 cm; 79 x 79 in
Photograph: Frank Youngs

below

87 **Cushion Pad** 1986
Wool and Dacron.
Pad of woven wool tubing made for
the Jim Partridge bench exhibited at
the *Britain in Vienna* week in
Kunsthalle, Vienna.
36 x 108 cm; 14 x 43 in
Collection: Jim Partridge
Photograph: Ann Sutton

88 **Materials Piece: Plastic**
1981
Darned fluorescent plastic thread,
mounted on perspex sheet.
One of a series in cotton, wool, linen,
plastic and silk, in which the aim was
to cram as many threads as possible
into a darn.
19.5 x 19.5 cm; 8 x 8 in
Collection: Ann Sutton
Photograph: David Cripps

opposite above
89 **Untitled experimental work
from Arundel studio** 1993

opposite below
90 **Too Long for its Space** 1993
Cotton and wool.
Loom-woven miniature.
29 x 33 cm; 11 x 13 in
Collection: Ann Sutton
Photograph: Ann Sutton

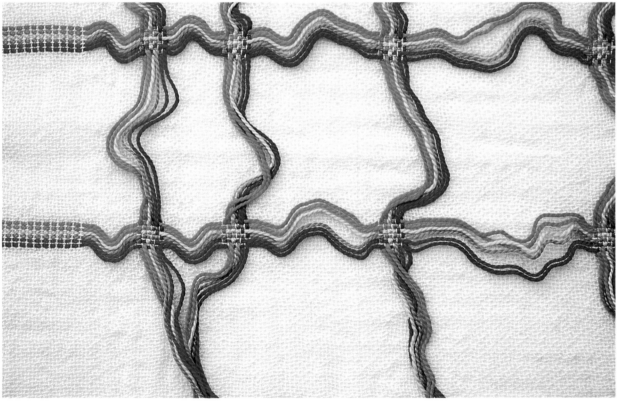

Ann Sutton: Constructive context
Susan Tebby

91 Abstract geometry
Substituting over five/under one in place of over three/under one at a certain point generates an asymmetric Greek Key design.
Photograph: Susan Tebby

Seeing the work of Ann Sutton for the first time is a revelatory experience. Subsequent viewing and reflection gradually reveal underlying, consistent patterns in her working processes more usually associated with the British constructivists of the 1950s onwards, rather than with mainstream textile design. The visual impact of Sutton's work, its structure, order and colour dynamics, have developed independently of, but in part parallel to the work of artists from what may appear, at first sight, to be markedly different fields of inquiry. Sutton's discovery – fortuitously early in her professional career – of like-minded individuals at the Barry Summer Schools endorsed her then current, but unsure thinking about possible alternative futures for woven textiles. While these facts have been briefly documented on other occasions,[1] including by Sutton herself,[2] there is a need for a more detailed look at these episodes and influences with the aim of gaining further insight into Sutton's conceptual development and unique working processes within a constructive context.

Sutton has often stressed the logic by which the content of her work progresses – a logic which is far more than that simply inherent in the weaving process itself. Sutton's participation in the Construction Course run by Kenneth Martin (1905–84) at Barry Summer School in the 1960s introduced to her for the first time the working ethos of Constructivism, simultaneously endorsing the viability of weave and yarn as a constructive medium with which to utilise and express certain abstract concepts and systems. Constructivism – a name coined in Russian literary circles in the 1920s – was neither a style nor a movement, but an intention and process towards the realisation of new (i.e. revolutionary) social ideals through the production of art and design.[3] Developments in science (for example, Einstein's *Theory of Relativity*), technology (particularly industrialisation and mass production, which had evolved much later in Russia than elsewhere in Europe) and mathematics (for example, to confirm new engineering principles) were central to this new socialisation of art and design.

92 Roman mosaic pavement
4th century AD
From a town house in Aldborough,
Yorkshire. Geometric scheme based
on a concept of fives in a 5 x 5
square grid.
Photograph: Susan Tebby

The legacy of Constructivism

These aims were nowhere more emphatically combined and channelled than in architecture. Thus construction and building in art, with concomitant materials (such as reinforced steel beams and bars, clear plastics, celluloid and acrylics, and later nylon) possessed a particular contemporary relevance. This was far removed from the traditions (or 'old order') of modelling in clay, cast bronze or stone carving. Part of the momentum towards the 'new order' was the emphasis given to science and mathematical concepts in published writings. The Russian brothers Naum Gabo (1890-1977) and Antoine Pevsner (1884-1962) wrote their now famous *Realist Manifesto* in 1920, affirming the new directions in art.[4]

Gabo came to England in 1935, settling in 1936, collaborating with abstract sculptors, including Henry Moore and Barbara Hepworth. Their respective views and differences were debated at length in the groups 'Axis' and 'Unit 1' and through the publication *Circle*.[5] However, the work of Moore and Hepworth and others, while being 'abstract', was perhaps more accurately termed 'abstraction' or 'abstracted' from nature or the figure, still expressed in the main through modelling and carving. Gabo subsequently found he had greater affinity with the geometric and non-mimetic ideas of Kenneth and Mary Martin (1907-69). Gabo's contribution to, and influence on the development of British art as a whole was highly significant.[6]

The year that Sutton entered Cardiff College of Art (1951), was a key point of departure in the development of constructivist work by both Kenneth and Mary Martin, as well as Victor Pasmore (1908-98). Although they had been making experimental abstract paintings and drawings since 1949, it was not until 1951 that Kenneth Martin made his first mobile, Mary Martin her first relief and Pasmore his first construction: these were their first three-dimensional works. While art that uses geometry as source and inspiration has been with us for millennia (91-93), never before had it been used as an exclusive constructing device for its own sake.[7]

During this period Kenneth Martin had begun studying extensively at the Science Museum, South Kensington. He became increasingly preoccupied by the possibilities offered by the mathematical models of the nineteenth century onwards. Martin's principal interest lay in the 'ruled surface' models that demonstrate how the articulation of a straight line traced in successive stages through space represents a three-dimensional curved-surface geometry. Most importantly these 'events' occurred in real time, in real space: they were four-dimensional. Martin's empirical investigations into how that space could be ordered, counter-ordered and reordered formed the basis of his kinetic screw mobiles from 1953 (94). At the same time Martin employed several well-known mathematical systems: in particular, the Fibonacci sequence[8] (95) and pendulum permutations,[9] both of which continue to be used by artists and designers today. Ann Sutton has made continual use of various pendulum permutations since they were first introduced to her by Martin – for example in *Black-to-White Pendulum Permutation* (1975) (96), which uses a pendulum permutation of six, or the hangings for Companies House, Cardiff, which use permutations of 10 and 15 (97, 98).

To give the concepts of time and space a physical reality, as the Russian constructivists had done in their time, Martin also had to consider the materials from which his constructions were made. Functional, industrially produced materials – rods, tubes, strips, washers, screw threads and so on – were put together strictly according to the generative system, the material itself affecting each elements' disposition in space relative to any and all other elements.[10] While the artist still has choices, the concept and system carry the logic of the work to its own conclusion, irrespective of the subjective wishes of the maker.

These, then, were some of the precepts that Ann Sutton encountered for the first time at Barry in the 1960s. To encourage students to move forward in this objective way of thinking and making, rather than having to rely on intuition or inspiration (which, of course, may never happen or arrive), Martin devised simple, practical experiments. First in symmetry – rotation, mirror reflection and imaging, and translation or glide symmetry[11] – and

93 Islamic stone carving
    Medieval period
From the portal to the caravanserai,
Sultanhani, Turkey.
Photograph: Susan Tebby

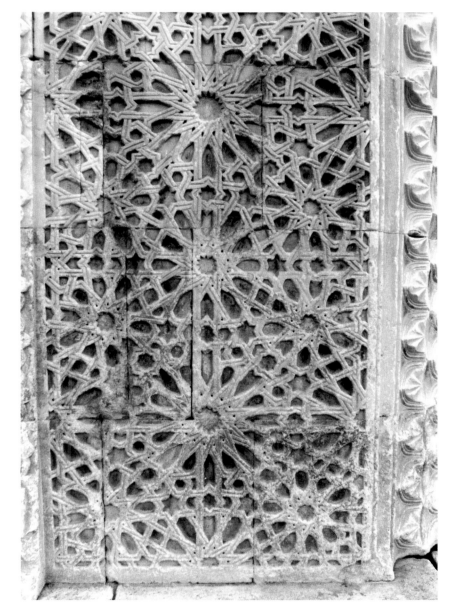

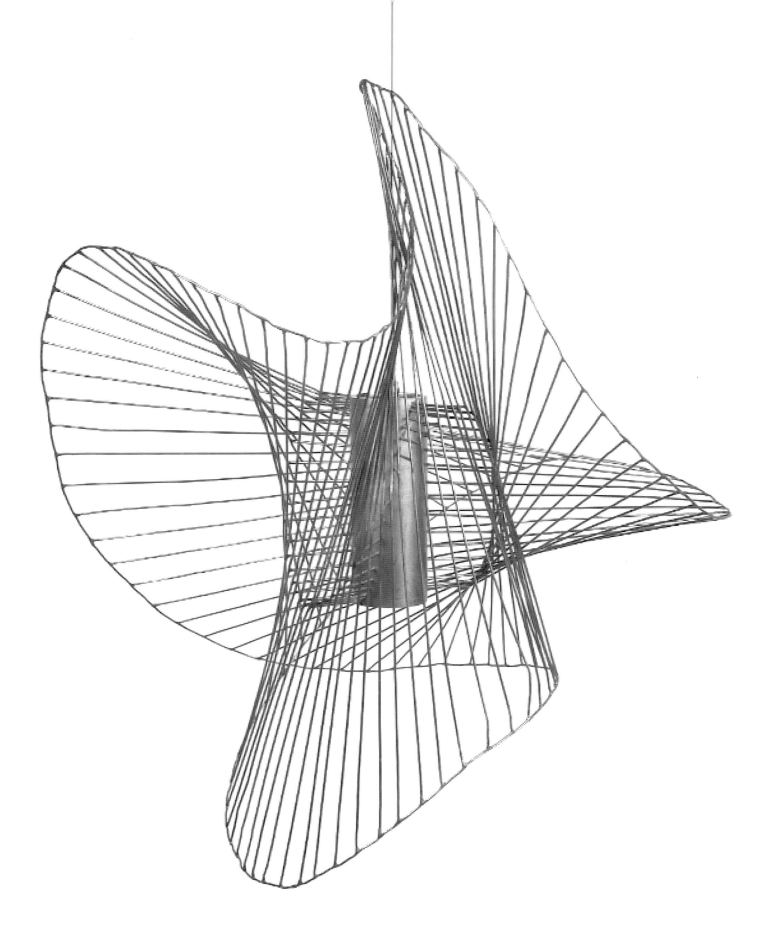

94 Kenneth Martin
Screw Mobile with Cylinder
1956
Phosphor bronze.
71 x 45 x 45 cm
Collection: Arts Council of England
Photograph: Mike Fear
© Courtesy Estate of Kenneth Martin

subsequently with pendulum permutations and other systematic procedures. Students were able to make objects without having to 'think up' a subject. The interest in the work was in exploring the logic of the system within the characteristics and properties of the material. Here, Sutton encountered the transparent properties of perspex and worked with the simple rotation of a half-cube. She recounts that having been ignored by Kenneth Martin for three days, she approached Peter Lowe (b.1939) his assistant (and a constructive artist in his own right), rather apprehensively, as to why this should be. Lowe responded by telling Sutton that Martin wanted to see what Sutton would make of the whole process as she had unwittingly selected similar elements to those that Mary Martin was currently investigating. Kenneth Martin did not wish to influence Sutton in coming to a resolution. Sutton's resultant double-sided relief was, in the event, unlike anything produced by Mary Martin. The work became self-supporting in the process, standing as it does on the base elements that lie either side of the dividing acrylic plane. One's eye does the travelling backwards and forwards, as it were, through the acrylic and back again, while the rotational system propels the half-cubes up and over the top. This already begins to sound like the logic of 'weave-thinking'.

Parallel worlds

By her own account, Sutton was exhilarated by the course at Barry, primarily because its precepts endorsed her own thinking, independently arrived at but still not fully formed. She became convinced that there was an equally viable way of working in her chosen field, one that did not have to remain within traditional confines, but one that could be governed by logical thinking, ordered independently by elements external to herself (and thus 'universal' in terms of communication). She was able to reinstate 'material', the 'stuff' of fabric as a substance with its own properties and characteristics that might be 'hard', 'transparent', 'coloured' or 'colourless', but with an independent life of its own. This clearly presented a positive, proactive challenge, entirely different from that of the submissive malleability of clay that Sutton so disliked. For Sutton, the constructive way of thinking and working had produced a coherent set of interrelationships between concept, system and material. The result was to manifest itself in a new wave of work – the beginning of freedom for her – in woven textiles.

Looking for key works among Sutton's vast output is not easy, as every phase of her development produces a key work as such; but certain works can be singled out because of the way in which they express the language of Constructivism so concisely. Her *Inverted Cube* (1973) is such a work. Whether she was aware of it at the time or not, this is a remarkable development into the field of topology, that branch of mathematics studying the properties of various kinds of spaces – in one, two, three and four dimensions – which do not fundamentally change under deformation. (Sutton would appreciate the irony that, before the advent of computer modelling, some of the hitherto successful ways to demonstrate these complex principles have been with clay!)[12] However, Sutton has 'flexed' nylon mesh inside out, outside in, on and within itself, constrained by the properties of nylon monofilament simultaneously with the characteristics of the material in semi-rigid cubic formation. The result defines new orientations in space, viewed through itself by the nature of the open-work mesh within the framework of the properties of the cube. *Extended Cube* (1968) (99) is an earlier variant.

Sutton forged links with other constructivist artists at that time, who increasingly referred to themselves as systematic constructive artists – a term that begins to appear to suit Sutton particularly well. These included Michael Kidner (b.1917), Jeffrey Steele (b.1931) and Richard Allen (1933–2000), all of whom had taught at Barry Summer School at the same time as Sutton and Martin. The 'Systems artists' brought together by Steele for the purposes of exhibiting and discourse during the 1970s and 1980s adhered to the principle that the system that generates the specific work is recoverable by means of analysis of the work.[13] It is often the case that such a system, or systems, can be recoverable from the work of Sutton, but there are always elements of surprise that defy such simplistic interpretation. Applying paint to the surface of woven material (which *has* been constructed according to a previous system) is not a system in, or by, itself. But the reasons for doing so are part of a continuing

95 Fibonacci sequences
abound in nature
Two consecutive numbers from the
series, 55 and 89, spiral left and
right respectively in this sunflower.
Photograph: Susan Tebby

96 **Black-to-White Pendulum Permutation** 1975

Own technique: unit textile, darned jute squares hooked with deep wool pile to form a rug.

130 x 130 x 5 cm; 51 x 51 x 2 in

Collection: Ann Sutton

Photograph: Sam Sawdon

**97 1–15 Pendulum
Permutation** 1976

Ann Sutton's own technique: knitted
and folded wool tube, darned in
squares and linked during
construction. Spectrum colours,
cross-pollinated horizontally. One of
two hangings commissioned by
Property Services Agency for
Companies House, Cardiff.
140 x 525 x 4 cm; 55 x 207 x 2 in
Collection: Hampshire County
Council

**98 1–10 Pendulum
Permutation** 1976

Ann Sutton's own technique: knitted
and folded tube, darned in squares
and linked during construction.
Subdued spectrum colours, cross-
pollinated horizontally. One of two
hangings commissioned by
Property Services Agency for
Companies House, Cardiff.
210 x 350 x 4 cm; 83 x 138 x 2 in
Collection: Hampshire County
Council

investigation into processes by which those very systems are expressed. Anton Ehrenzweig (1901–66), the psychologist, said at an open forum discussion at Barry: 'Material is not the important part. It is what goes on in here [tapping his head] that matters. The work of Ann Sutton perfectly exemplifies this.'[14]

The logic of systems

While the teaching and influence of Kenneth Martin may have been a primary impetus for, and endorsement of, Sutton's early development, she has said that she has more affinity with the work of Mary Martin. Mary Martin's work was concerned with what happens between the outermost surface of the relief and the wall on which it sits, or from which it departs. In other words, the relief can be described as a multi-layered work with pre-determined thicknesses, set in a relatively shallow space. The analogy with woven textile becomes possible at this point. Mary Martin used, among other systems, the 'golden section',[15] root rectangles[16] and pendulum permutations, sometimes in isolation, but more often using the same system more than once in the same work. Her focus on material, especially the reflective surface of stainless steel – *Compound Rhythms with Blue* (1966) (100) – allows for the unexpected to occur. Due to the nature of the system (here she employed pendulum permutations) the 'blue' of the title is applied only to those surfaces determined by the system, which happen to be those at right angles to the viewer. Consequently, the blue is only seen in reflection, which constantly change as one approaches or moves away from the work.[17] The 'now you see it, now you don't' has some parallels with both the works with the 'invisible squares technique' as well as the double-woven structures of Sutton where woven elements or membranes travel behind and then in front of the surface. Vestiges of colour from the underlying threads penetrate between the network of top-lying threads, making visible, as it were, ghost colours that then reappear, but modified by another, crossing colour. Sutton's serial woven structures of 1995, shown in the exhibition *No Cheating* at Winchester in 1995, which concentrate on satin (vertical/warp) and sateen (horizontal/weft) surfaces, also catch the light intermittently according to one's relative position, while the elements themselves physically appear and disappear according to the determinants of the generating system (101).

99 **Extended Cube** 1968

Nylon monofilament.
Miniature textile sculpture. Versions
were made in both transparent and
black nylon monofilament. Exhibited
at the *First International Exhibition
of Miniature Textiles* in 1974.
13.5 x 13.5 x 13.5 cm; 5 x 5 x 5 in
Photograph: Ann Sutton

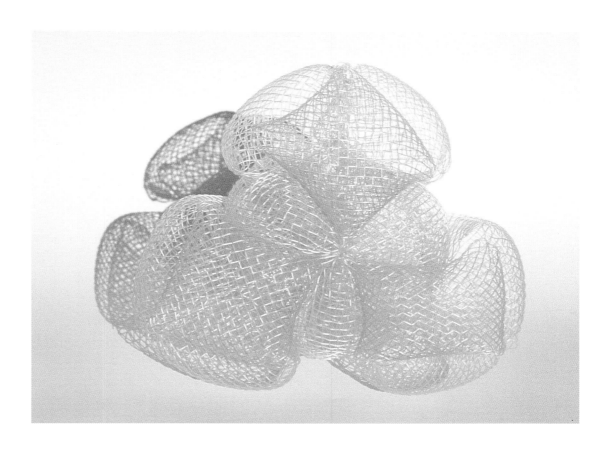

Mary Martin
100 **Compound Rhythms with Blue**
1966
Stainless steel, formica and wood.
107 x 107 x 7.5 cm; 41.5 x 42 x 3 in
Collection: Arts Council of England
© Courtesy Estate of Mary Martin

Sutton was intrigued to discover from Kenneth Martin that Mary Martin had also been very much involved with weaving during the 1930s and 1940s (eventually becoming Head of Weaving at Chelmsford School of Art). Mary Martin had rarely mentioned this part of her professional career, seeing it as separate from her concerns as a constructivist artist. But on looking at some of her drawings (102) involving pendulum permutations, one is struck by their nature. Here, the origins of what might be a weave notation are transcribed partly as a code for orientating elements across a surface, defining their order and position in space and articulating the elements themselves as they progress. Sutton's interest in this work, this coding, is understandable. While Sutton rarely makes drawings of this kind, her concerns are not dissimilar: order and disorder/reorder; play and interplay; rhythm and counter-rhythm.

Sutton has professed herself not to be a mathematician, just as the Martins and most other constructive artists have also done. Yet her fascination with numerical ordering and numbers continues: she uses them as determinants and devices precisely because of their almost infinite potential within a finite framework. At the same time, the methods by which permutations can be generated by computer leaves Sutton free to move ahead once more with other concerns. Sutton continues to liken her use of systems to the essential use of rules within musical composition. Mozart and Bach may be regarded by many as the most inventive of their times, yet both adhere strictly to the rigorous rules of composition, each with attendant systems of key, harmony and dissonance, pitch and melody. It is not the search for the unique in itself, but the intelligent and creative application of such systems, their successful integration one with another, within a logical framework, that makes each work unique. Such is the path of the work of Ann Sutton.

101 **White Linen Permutations**
1995
Linen.
Series of six miniature textiles, shown
at the solo *No Cheating* exhibition
at the Winchester Gallery,
Winchester School of Art.
25 x 25 cm; 10 x 10 in
Collection: Ann Sutton
Photograph: James Newell

Notes

1 *Ann Sutton: Textiles*, exhibition catalogue, with essay by Peter Dormer; Norrköping Konstmuseum, Sweden, 1985 and Bellew Publishing, London, 1985.

2 *Textile Art and Constructive Tradition*, recorded notes from textile artists at a seminar held to coincide with the exhibition detailed in note 1, Norrköping Konstmuseum, 1985.

3 Stephen Bann (ed.), *The Documents of 20th Century Art: The Tradition of Constructivism*, Thames and Hudson, London, 1974; see also W. Rotzler, *Constructive Concepts*, ABC Edition Zurich, Zurich, 1977; G. Rickey, *Constructivism: Origins and Evolution*, George Braziller Inc, New York, 1967, revised edition 1995.

4 N. Gabo, H. Read and L. Martin, *Gabo*, Lund Humphries, London, 1957. The *Manifesto* is quoted in full, a facsimile in Russian with English translation, from p.151.

5 J. L. Martin, B. Nicholson and N. Gabo, *Circle*, Faber and Faber, London, 1937; reprinted London 1971.

6 Gabo has, so far, been the only artist to have had three major exhibitions at the Tate Gallery: 1966, 1976, 1987. Alistair McAlpine was commissioned by the Tate Gallery to build Gabo's *Revolving Torsion* in the grounds of St Thomas's Hospital, Westminster Bridge. The kinetic fountain was completed in 1975 to coincide with the second exhibition. See also *Art Monthly*, no.4, February 1977 for a detailed discussion with Gabo about the evolution of the work.

7 The first critical appraisal of the work of the British Abstract Artists, as they called themselves in the first few years, appeared in *Nine Abstract Artists*, by Lawrence Alloway, Tiranti, London, 1957.

8 Fibonacci represents the conflated name of Leonardo of Pisa, Filius (= son of) Bonacci, who was the first to write down in 1202, in his *Liber Abaci*, the sequence of numbers that bears his name, and to explain its mathematical reasoning. In essence, any number in the sequence is the sum of the two preceding it: thus, number 1 is the sum of 0+1, and so the sequence may be computed (0,1),1,2,3,5,8,13,21 etc. to infinity. For other artists' and scientists' interest in this and related systems, see G. Kepes (ed.), *Module, Symmetry, Proportion*, George Braziller Inc, New York, 1966, and particularly E. Ehrenkranz, 'Modular materials and design flexibility', pp 118–27.

9 A pendulum permutation is an array of numbers the order of which in the first row is permutated in the second and successive rows, by alternately 'swinging' the numbers right and then left until the original order of the first line is regained. Thus the sequence 1,2,3,4,5 is permutated 2,4,5,3,1; 4,3,1,5,2 and so on until 1,2,3,4,5 is regained in the sixth row. Different quantities permutate 'out' in a different number of rows. See S. Tebby, *Patterns of Organisation in Constructive Art*, Leicester, 1983.

10 A comprehensive exposition, with a comparative table of the generating systems, principles, materials and proportionate systems for a series of works by Kenneth Martin was first published (with editorial revision) in the research journal *Leonardo*, vol.1, October 1968; the full unedited version was published in 'Construction and Change', *Kenneth Martin, Retrospective*, exhibition catalogue, Tate Gallery, 1975, pp. 30–41.

11 See H. Weyl, *Symmetry*, Princeton University Press, Princeton, 1952.

12 The Science Museum, London currently has on show a number of mathematical models in plaster, casts of originals modelled in clay.

13 *Systems*, exhibition catalogue, Whitechapel Art Gallery, with an introductory essay by S. Bann, London, 1972.

14 Anton Ehrenzweig's comment in 1965 or 1966 about the implied need for an intelligent response may be compared with the comments of the critic John Russell, in *Painting 64-67*, Arts Council exhibition and catalogue (1968) of the same title: '... once again ... Kenneth Martin ..., who, both as artist and teacher first showed us that thought-out and cerebral art were not the same ....'. See also Anton Ehrenzweig, *The Hidden Order of Art*, University of California Press, Berkeley and Los Angeles, 1967 for his further discussions about abstraction and perception in art.

15 Jay Hambidge, *The Elements of Dynamic Symmetry*, Yale University Press, New Haven, 1926, reprinted London 1967, has been an influential book for constructivist artists and others of successive periods, much used by the Martins in their teaching. The 'golden section' is a proportional system: the relationship of the shorter (line, area, volume) to the longer (line, area, volume), is as the longer is to the whole (i.e. the shorter + the longer). A root 2, usually written $\sqrt{2}$, rectangle is formed by taking the diagonal of the square as the length of the rectangle projected on to the side of the square. If the length of the side of the original square is 1, the diagonal is 1.414: the square root of 2 (by Pythagoras). Successive root rectangles, $\sqrt{3}$, $\sqrt{4}$ (a double square), $\sqrt{5}$ etc., take the diagonal of the preceding rectangle as the new side-length on the original square.

16 See *Mary Martin, Retrospective*, exhibition catalogue, Tate Gallery, 1984.

17 See 'Reflections' by Mary Martin, pp 95–100, in Anthony Hill (ed.), *Directions in Art, Theory and Aesthetics*, Faber and Faber, London, 1968, for a lucid account of this work and its philosophical context.

Mary Martin
102 **Permutation of Six** *c.*1966
Ink on paper. 36 sections mounted on a
single sheet of paper.
45.7 x 45.7 cm
© Courtesy Estate of Mary Martin
Photograph: Susan Tebby

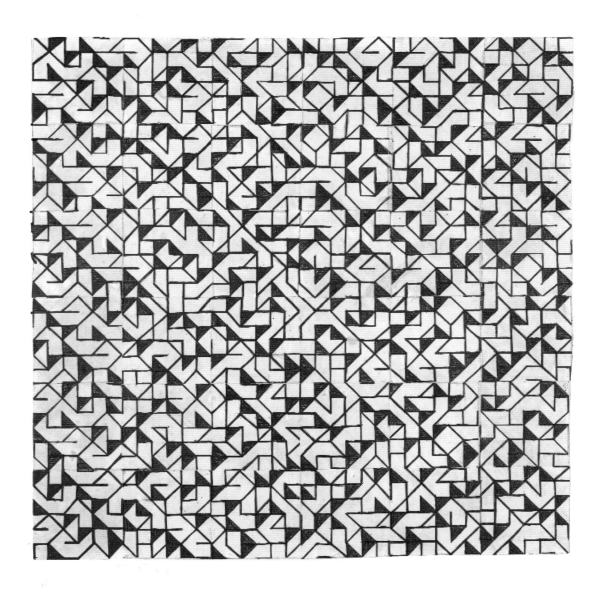

Recent Work

103 **Six Layers of Linen, Rotating** 1995
Linen.
Series of miniature textiles with
several colour permutations, shown at the
solo *No Cheating* exhibition at the
Winchester Gallery, Winchester School of Art.
21 x 21 cm; 8 x 8 in
Collection: Ann Sutton
Photograph: James Newell

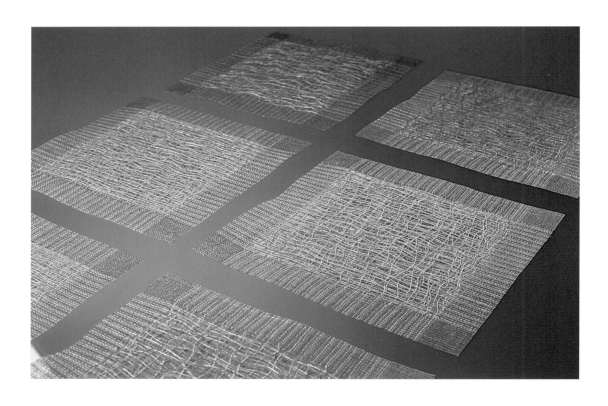

104 Spectrum Patches 1995

Wool.

Series of six miniature textiles, shown at
the solo *No Cheating* exhibition at the
Winchester Gallery, Winchester School
of Art.

21 cm; 8 in wide with varying lengths

Collection: Ann Sutton

Photograph: James Newell

105 **Frozen Fabric: Small**
Sprayed Plain 1996
Cotton cloth strip and acrylic paint.
25 x 25 cm; 10 x 10 in
Collection: Ann Sutton
Photograph: David Cripps

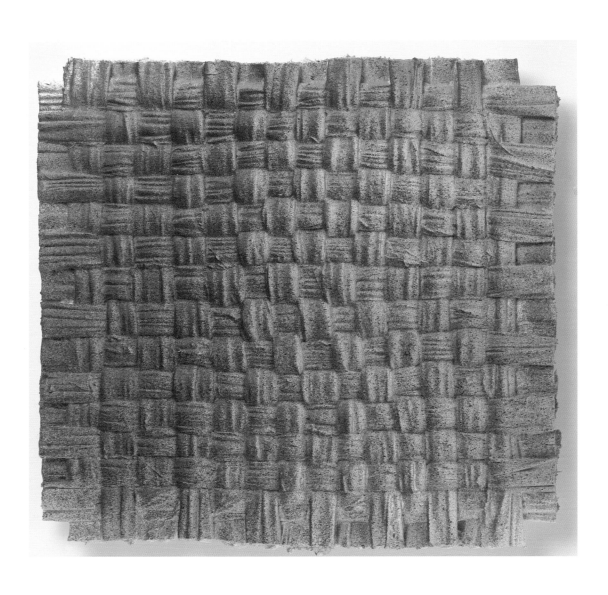

106 Interior Scheme 1998

Carpet and worsted wool upholstery.
Textile. Ann Sutton was appointed Project
Artist for the conversion of Eastleigh Town
Hall into a new dance centre, The Point.
Her designs included gold and silver
architectural detailing, murals, carpets and
special lettered upholstery.
Collection: Hampshire County Council
Photograph: Ann Sutton

107 Linen Morphing to Gold 2001

Linen and lurex.
A 24-harness computer-driven loom
transmutes these hangings from linen warp
(faced satin) to gold weft (faced sateen).
Various sizes:
195–280 long x 210–300 cm wide;
77–110 x 83–118 in
Photograph: David Cripps

108 **Movement Meshes** 2001

One of a series of ink-on-paper drawings that record the effect of movement on a carefully spaced grid of horizontal and vertical lines. The title, *Old Porsche – Oxford to Banbury,* reveals the journey on which these 'on-the-move' drawings were made.

15 x 21 cm; 6 x 8 in

Photograph: David Cripps

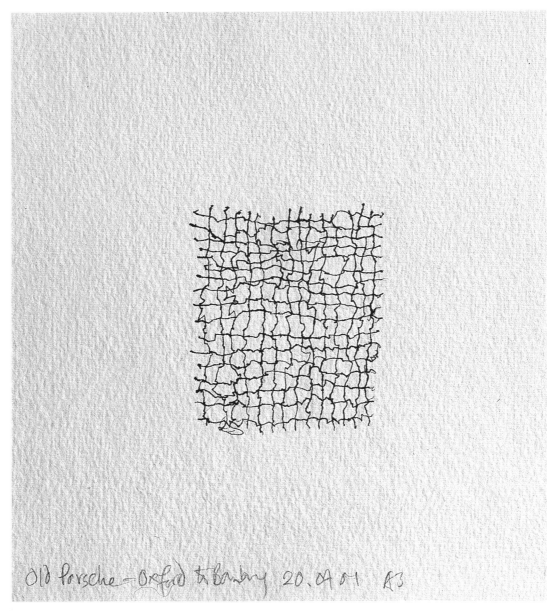

Old Porsche — Oxford to Banbury 20.04.01

109 **Disappearing Honeycomb**
2002
Linen.
In this series of woven hangings the
honeycomb patterns gradually become
plain weave.
Approximately 200 x 37 cm; 79 x 15 in
Photograph: David Cripps

Glossary

Dobby loom
A loom with a mechanism for controlling up to 40 shafts and an unlimited number of picks in the design repeat. The dobby mechanism can either be mechanical or electronic. Modern electronic dobby looms are computer controlled.

Double-woven
The simultaneous production of two component woven layers of cloth that can be held together by: (a) integral stitching threads; (b) the intersection of warp or weft threads from the two layers; (c) the interchanging of the component layers; (d) the combining of warp or weft threads from the two layers to make one layer.

Filament
A fibre of indefinite or extreme length such as found naturally in silk. Manufactured yarns are extruded into filaments of various sizes.

Monofilament
A yarn composed of a single long fibre as in silk.

Selvedge
The lengthwise edge of a fabric running parallel to the warp.

Tapestry
A method of producing a pictorial weaving with discontinuous wefts of various colours that are woven back and forth over specific areas on the warp.

Warp
Threads travelling lengthways in a fabric as woven.

Weft (filling)
Threads travelling widthways in a fabric as woven.

Chronology

1935 Born in North Staffordshire, England

1951–6 Awarded National Diploma of Design (Embroidery and Woven Textile Design), Cardiff College of Art

1956–63 In charge of the Woven Textile Department at West Sussex College of Art. Also ran many workshops and summer schools, including Barry Summer School, Wales

1957 Membership of Contemporary Applied Arts (was British Crafts Centre)

1963–5 Part-time lecturer at Croydon College of Art

1964 Married furniture maker, John Makepeace

1964–78 Director of John Makepeace Limited (interior design/furniture/textiles)

1965 Styled, commissioned and marketed own range of bedcovers

1966 Cottage industry production of cushions (for Heals, Dunns and Liberty & Company)

1967–78 Consultant to various Welsh woollen mills

1970 Winner of *Sculpture '70* Welsh Arts Council Competition for *Bristle Box*

1971 Royal Society of Arts Scholarship: Nigeria and Morocco

1972 Selected as Member of Contemporary Applied Arts (was British Crafts Centre)

1972 Consultancy: Camden Art Centre, *Woven Structures*

1972 Member of Grants for Special Projects Committee: Crafts Council

1974 1975 World Crafts Council Conference, Toronto and United States

1974 Initiated *First International Exhibition of Miniature Textiles*: British Crafts Centre and world tour (and three subsequent exhibitions)

1975 Member of Royal Society of Arts

1976 Chaired Fibre Programme, World Crafts Council Conference, Mexico

1977 Elected Fellow of the Society of Industrial Artists and Designers (now Chartered Society of Designers)

1978 Major Crafts Bursary Award, Crafts Council

1978 Adviser to Crown Wallcoverings: exhibition and competition

1979 Initiated *The Art of Craft* seminar, Contemporary Art Society and the Crafts Council, RIBA, London

1980 Presented five-part series on BBC TV called *The Craft of the Weaver*

1980 Initiated Arundel Textile Summer School with John Hinchcliffe

1980 Initiated *Weave at Sea* cruise, P&O Lines

1981 Chaired convention on *The Miniature Textile*, University of Athens, Georgia, United States (also Las Vegas and Houston)

1981–4 Member of Southern Arts (RAA) Visual Arts Panel

1982 Invited to plan exhibition of own choice at John Hansard Gallery, University of Southampton, *Attitudes to Tapestry*

1983 Buyer (paintings/sculpture) for Contemporary Art Society

1983 Reinstated the Craft Fund for Contemporary Art Society: first buyer

1984 Major Crafts Bursary Award: Southern Arts

1984–5 Consultant designer and coordinator of *The Wales Collection* (furnishing fabrics and children's wear) for the Wales Craft Council/Welsh Woollen Association

1985 Lecture tour, Australia (Australian Crafts Council and British Council)

1986 Visiting lecturer, Konstfackskolan, Stockholm, Sweden

1986 Lecture tour, United States and Canada (Rhode Island School of Art and Design, Cranbrook, Banff)

1986 Teacher in conjunction with solo exhibition, Konstfachskolan, Stockholm, Sweden

1987 Designed collections for Early's of Witney.

1987–90 Founded the Ann Sutton School of Weave Design, to train students from the United States, Norway, Sweden, Ireland, New Zealand, The Netherlands, South Africa, Japan and the United Kingdom

1988 Consultant to the EEC: *Weaving in the Philippines* – a report on export potential

1988 International judge, *Fashion Fabric Design* contest, Tokyo

1988 Lectured and designed (with Junichi Arai), Japan

1988–9 Adviser to Sophis Computer Design Systems, Belgium

1988–90 Member of Steering Group, *PerCent for Art*, Arts Council

1989 Initiated a gallery trail for the Arundel Festival (50 temporary art galleries)

1989 Initiated/commissioned *Kotatsus*: UK textile craftsmen, for Taido Living, Tokyo

1989–90 Produced two collections each year with Junichi Arai, Japan: evening dress fabrics – working in woven textiles, raschel, warp-knit, embroidery, finishing

1990–1 Project Director, Winchester Cathedral *New Textiles*, with other British textile artists and Issey Mikaye

1990–present Part-time lecturer, Woven and Embroidered Textiles, Royal College of Art

1990–present Freelance furnishing designs for Ralph Lauren, Fieldcrest Cannon, etc.

1991 Member of the Order of the British Empire (MBE)

1991 Visiting lecturer, Haystack School for Crafts, Maine, United States

1992–? Vision Director, S I G H T SPECIFIC applied art agency

1994 Keynote address, Weavers Guild of America: Convergence 94, Minneapolis

1995 Examining Committee, Textile School, Rhode Island School of Design

1995   Judge, Swiss Design Prize, Solothum,
        Switzerland

1995   Consultancy to the Crafts Council of Ireland
        Floor-coverings conference

1995-6 Project Artist, Stage 1: The Point, Eastleigh
        Town Hall

1996   Ideas Consultant, Stage 1: Museum of Science
        & Industry, Manchester (new gallery)

1997   Consultancy, Stage 2: Museum of Science &
        Industry, Manchester (new gallery, advising,
        commissioning, buying art)

1998   Ann Sutton Foundation for International
        Weave Design Research initiated

2001   Consultant and Artist, Stage 2: The Point,
        Eastleigh Town Hall

2001   Selector, Chelsea Crafts Fair (Crafts Council)

2002   Ann Sutton Foundation for International
        Weave Design Research opened

2002   Prepared body of work for gallery showing

Selected exhibitions

Solo exhibitions

1969 *Ann Sutton: Textiles*, British Crafts Centre, London

1970 *Textile Images on Paper*, Victoria and Albert Museum (Circulation Department), London

1975 *Ann Sutton: Textiles*, British Crafts Centre, London

1975 *Architecture & Living*, Wohnen Design, Düsseldorf, Germany

1979 *Work in Progress*, Crafts Council, London and tour (organised by Crafts Council)

1984 *Ann Sutton Textiles*, Anatol Orient Gallery, London

1985 *Ann Sutton Textiles*, Norrköpings Konstmuseum, Sweden (Southern Arts and British Council)

1986 *Ann Sutton Textiles*, Borås Textilmuseet, Borås, Sweden

1986 *Ann Sutton*, Konstfackskolan, Stockholm, Sweden

1987 *Ann Sutton Textiles*, Carmarthen Library and touring Wales

1995 *No Cheating*, serial woven studies, Southern Arts Touring Exhibition Service

Group exhibitions

1962 *Seven Artists*, Hove Museum, Sussex

1963 *Designer Craftsmen '63*, Herbert Art Gallery, Coventry, organised by John Makepeace

1970 *Beutlich, Collingwood & Sutton*, Dennis Croneen Gallery, Sydney, Australia

1970 *1st, 3rd and 4th International Exhibitions of Miniature Textiles*, British Crafts Centre, London and world tour

1973 *Hand and Machine*, part of *Europalia '73*, Design Centre, Brussels, Belgium

1973 *The Craftsman's Art* (Crafts Council), Victoria and Albert Museum, London

1974 *Sutton/Treen*, touring exhibition, organised by Crafts Council

1977 *Ceramics and Textiles: British Cultural Festival*, Mehre Shah Gallery, Teheran, Iran and tour organised by British Council

1977 *International Tapestry Triennale* (invited British exhibitor), Lodz, Poland

1980 *The Craft of the Weaver*, British Crafts Centre, London

1980 *Contemporary British Crafts*, Sotheby's, London

1981 *International Triennale of Tapestries*, Central Museum of Textiles, Lodz, Poland

1985 *Constructivist Clothing*, Oxford Gallery, Oxford (with Diana Hawkins and Caroline Broadhead)

1987 *Wall to Wall*, Cornerhouse, Manchester and touring (Sutton wrote part of the catalogue)

1988 *Classics in the Crafts*, Crafts Council, London

1998 *The Pleasures of Peace*, Sainsbury Centre for the Visual Arts, Norwich

2003 *Show5 – Ann Sutton*, Retrospective, The Crafts Council, London

Selected commissions

1972 Crafts Council, *Floor Pad* for *The Craftsman's Art Rim for Floor Pad* later purchased for the Crafts Council Collection

1974 Ahrends, Burton & Koralek, logical colour scheme for Keble College, Oxford

1975 Liberty & Company, *Love Seat*

1976 Department of the Environment, two hangings for Companies House, Cardiff *1–10 Pendulum Permutation* and *1–15 Pendulum Permutation*

1973 New Law Courts, Crewe, Cheshire, Lay-Light

1979 Crafts Council, *Work in Progress,* a small didactic exhibition

1980 Mercantile & General Reinsurance, three untitled hangings at the entrance to their headquarters, Moorgate, London (commissioned by Denis Lasdun and Partners)

1983 Crafts Council, flags for headquarters (in competition)

1984 Delaunay Limited, constructivist textiles for batch production

2002 Dame Stephanie Shirley, book cover cloth

Collections

Public collections

Finland
Museum of Modern Art, Helsinki

Sweden
National Museum, Stockholm
Norrköpings Konstmuseum, Norrköpings
Borås Tekomuseum, Borås

United Kingdom
Victoria and Albert Museum, London (24 pieces)
Lotherton Hall, City of Leeds Museums and Galleries
National Museum of Wales, Cardiff
The Crafts Council, London
Department of the Environment, Wales

Private collections

Qatar
The Crown Prince of Qatar

Elsewhere
Various private collections in Europe, the United States
and Australia

Selected bibliography

Adamczewski, Fiona, *Designer Textiles: Stitching for Interiors*, David & Charles, Newton Abbot, Devon, 1987

Bann, S., *Systems*, exh.cat., Whitechapel Art Gallery, London, 1971

Bann, Stephen (ed.), *The Documents of 20th Century Art: The Tradition of Constructivism*, Thames and Hudson, London, 1974

Benn, Elizabeth, 'Keep taking the tablets', *Daily Telegraph*, 5 March 1975

Brosterman, Norman, *Inventing Kindergarten*, Harry N. Abrams, New York, 1997

Constantine, Mildred and Lenor Larsen, Jack, *Beyond Craft: The Art Fabric*, Van Nostrand Reinhold Company, New York, 1972

Cooper, Emmanuel, 'Travelling craft', *Morning Star*, 28 April 1980

Dormer, Peter, *Ann Sutton Textiles*, exh.cat., Bellew Publishing Company, London, 1985

Dormer, Peter (ed.), *The Culture of Craft*, Manchester University Press, Manchester and New York, 1997

Ehrenkranz, E., 'Modular materials and design flexibility', in Kepes, G. (ed.), *Module, Symmetry, Proportion*, George Braziller Inc, New York, 1966

Ehrenzweig, A., *The Hidden Order of Art*, University of California Press, Berkeley and Los Angeles, 1967

Gabo, N., Read, H. and Martin, L., *Gabo*, Lund Humphries, London, 1957

Gillett, John, *No Cheating*, exh.cat., The Winchester Gallery, Winchester, 1995

Glynn, Prudence, 'Design: An eye on the future in a setting of the past', *The Times*, 14 April 1977

Hambidge, Jay, *The Elements of Dynamic Symmetry*, Yale University Press, New Haven, 1926, reprinted London, 1967

Harrod, Tanya, *The Crafts in Britain in the 20th Century*, Yale University Press, New Haven, 1999

Heydeman, Elizabeth, 'Review of ideas in weaving', *Journal for Weavers, Spinners and Dyers*, no.152, October 1989

Hill, Anthony, *Directions in Art, Theory and Aesthetics*, Faber and Faber, London, 1968

Kenneth Martin, Retrospective, exh.cat., Tate Gallery, London, 1975

Kepes, G. (ed.), *Module, Symmetry, Proportion*, George Braziller Inc, New York, 1966

Martin, J. L., Nicholson, B. and Gabo, N., *Circle*, Faber and Faber, London, 1937, reprinted London, 1971

Mary Martin, Retrospective, exh.cat., Tate Gallery, London, 1984

McLucas, Clifford, *Ann Sutton Gweadwaith*, Dyfed Cultural Services, Wales, 1985

Rickey, G., *Constructivism: Origins and Evolution*, George Braziller Inc, New York 1967; (revised edition) 1995

Rotzler, Willy, *Constructive Concepts*, ABC Editions, Zurich, 1977, 1989

Sutton, Ann, *The Craftsman's Art*, exh.cat., Crafts Council (Textiles Section), 1973

122   Sutton, Ann, 'Weaving for fun and profit', *Crafts*, November/December 1978

Sutton, Ann, Various articles as British correspondent, *American Fabrics & Fashion*, 1981–4

Sutton, Ann, *The Structure of Weaving*, Hutchinson, London, 1982

Sutton, Ann, 'Through the eye of the needle', *Crafts* (10th Anniversary Edition), 1983

Sutton, Ann, *Colour-and-Weave*, Bellew Publishing Company, London, 1984

Sutton, Ann, 'Textiles', *Design Brief*, no.12, vol.2, March 1985

Sutton, Ann, *British Craft Textiles*, William Collins & Sons, London, 1985

Sutton, Ann, 'Art of fine fabrics', *Sussex Life*, March 1986

Sutton, Ann, 'Designing fabrics for fashion', *Handwoven*, July 1986

Sutton, Ann, *The Textiles of Wale*s, Bellew Publishing Company, London, 1987

Sutton, Ann (ed.), *Falcot's Treatise of Weaving*, McDonald/Bellew, London, 1990

Sutton, Ann, 'Junichi Arai', *International Textiles*, 1992

Sutton, Ann with Carr, Richard, *Tartans*, Bellew Publishing Company, London, 1984

Sutton, Ann with Collingwood, Peter and St Aubyn Hubbard, Geraldine, *The Craft of the Weaver*, BBC Publications, London, 1979

Sutton, Ann and Evans, Kim, 'Working in Oxfordshire', *Crafts*, November/December, 1974

Sutton, Ann with Holtom, Pat, *Tablet-Weaving*, Batsford, London, 1973

Sutton, Ann with Sheehan, Diane, *Ideas in Weaving*, Batsford (United Kingdom) and Interweave (United States), 1989

Tebby, S., *Patterns of Organization in Constructive Art*, Leicester, 1983

Vaizey, Marina, '*Design 70*, Oxford Gallery' (review), *Arts*, 28 February 1970

Westfall, Carol D., 'Ann Sutton: Pushing parameters', *Fiberarts Magazine*, 1996

Weyl, H., *Symmetry*, Princeton University Press, Princeton, 1952

Acknowledgements

For most of my weaving life I have been fortunate to have had lovely assistants in my studio, who have not only become good friends but have also enabled me to produce work in quantities for exhibitions. In chronological order: Mary; Stuart Houghton and Angela Fell; the Mollington team, including Rose, Sylvia, Marlene and Anne; Elizabeth Milner; Joanne Boxall; Lucy Willemse. (The last three were better weavers than I will ever be.) If I have left someone out, forgive me. I am very grateful for all the careful attention that my assistant friends have added to my work over the years: I could not have managed without them.

Ann Sutton

Index of works